BOLLYWOOD

The Indian Cinema Story

Nasreen Munni Kabir

First published in August 2001 by Channel 4 Books
an imprint of Pan Macmillan Ltd
20 New Wharf Road, London N1 9RR, Basingstoke and Oxford.

Associated companies throughout the world.

www.panmacmillan.com

ISBN 0 7522 1943 X

9 8 7 6 5 4 3 2 1

A CIP catalogue record for this book is available from the British Library.

Designed and typeset by seagulls
Printed by Mackays of Chatham plc, Chatham, Kent

Picture credits: Page 1 - National Film Archives of India, Pune, Hussaini
Bhai. Page 2 - Dev Anand/Navketan; Randhir Kapoor/RK Films. Page 3 -
Iqbal Khan/Shaukat Khan; Mehboob Productions Pvt Ltd; RK Films.
Page 4 - Lata Mangeshkar courtesy of Peter Chappell, HMV, India. Page 5 -
S. Mukherji Productions; Dev Anand/Navketan; RK Films. Page 6 - Dilip
Sircar/New Theatres; Joy Roy/Bimal Roy Productions; Arun Dutt/Guru Dutt
Films Pvt Ltd; Bombay Talkies. Page 7 - Iqbal Khan/Shaukat Khan; Mehboob
Productions Pvt Ltd; Farouque Rattansay; BR Films. Page 8 - Ramesh Sippy;
Hrishikesh Mukherjee; Mani Ratnam/Madras Talkies; Khalid Mohamed.

The publishers have made every effort to trace the owners of these
photographs, and apologise for any omissions.

Back cover portraits of Hritik Roshan, Aishwarya Rai,
Amitabh Bachchan and Juhi Chawla © Gautam Rajadhyaksha.

CONTENTS

FOREWORD

by Amitabh Bachchan

Most of what we read about Hindi cinema is so caustic it burns through the paper it is written on. It is a delight therefore going through Nasreen Kabir's impressions on a medium which is fast becoming an international phenomenon – something that we always knew and believed in, and something that the rest of the world is discovering rather rapidly.

The uniqueness of Hindi cinema has been its content. From its very inception, its content has remained unchanged. This very factor, that has borne endless criticism and ridicule, now provides platforms for intellectual debate, has entered educational curriculum and become a forbearer of the nation's identity. It has survived almost a hundred years and is still growing. If over a billion people love and patronise Hindi cinema, it must be doing something right. All credit then to Nasreen Kabir and her attempt to delve a little deeper into the reasons for this. I am often asked, 'When did Hindi films start being taken seriously?' And I have always responded with, 'Hindi films were always serious business. It's wonderful to see them getting serious comment now.'

I feel particularly gratified that Nasreen brings about this much-needed commentary through this absorbing book of hers. She has always been a staunch believer in everything that Hindi cinema has offered. Her earlier involvement through the television series *Movie Mahal* and the books she wrote on Guru Dutt and Javed Akhtar reflect the dexterity with which she has subtly analysed the medium, revealing to the viewer and the reader an aspect which could perhaps have gone unnoticed. She has understood human psychology – and what is cinema but just that? Her craft in this latest presentation has, I can safely say, only improved.

I hope every Hindi film lover gets to read this book, not just because it will be most rewarding, but because it deserves to be read.

Amitabh Bachchan, May 2001

INTRODUCTION

It wasn't difficult for Channel 4 Books to persuade me to write about my favourite subject. Since I began studying Hindi films in 1978, I realized it was easier for me to forget an important personal anniversary than to forget the name of S.D. Burman's first film, Nargis's dialogue in *Mother India*, in which films V.K. Murthy worked as an assistant cameraman or whose voice was used for the 'yahoo' cry in the famous *Junglee* song. Trying to find out everything there was to know about certain films has been an adventure. Then finally realizing that no matter how much you think you have discovered, the great films always hold something back, revealing bits of themselves according to one's changing experience and emotional state. And this is also true of the best of Indian cinema.

Living in Britain and in France nearly all my life has meant that Hindi film music and Hindi films have been the main cultural link to India, where I was born. I soon found out that this experience and link was shared by millions of people, whose origins are in the subcontinent but who have settled all around the world. It isn't surprising that so many millions are captivated by Indian cinema. There is something unique about a Hindi film – its innocent idea of romance, emphasis on family values, reverence of old world customs, colourful sets, marvelously moving music and dance, and most importantly, its skills in neatly resolving the conflict between good and bad - that makes one wish that life was vaguely like that.

quote!

In the early 1980s, when Hindi films were regarded as being of marginal interest in the West, labels like 'Bollywood' - dividing opinion among Indian film practitioners and audiences about its usage – did not exist, Channel 4's Sue Woodford, the first Commissioning Editor for Multicultural Programmes, made sure that Indian films were shown on a regular basis. Over the years, this became a tradition on Channel 4 and subsequent Commissioning Editors, including Farrukh Dhondy, Yasmin Anwar, Patrick Younge and Stevan Keane, never failed to include Hindi films in their output. I was lucky that they gave me the brief to 'curate' the annual Hindi film seasons and this work led on to my producing and directing long series on the Hindi cinema including *Movie Mahal*, *Lata in Her Own Voice*, *Follow that Star*, *How to Make it Big in Bollywood* and *How to Make a Bollywood Movie*. Channel 4 has played a big part in bringing Hindi films to the attention of the mainstream in Britain, and I feel very fortunate to have been involved in that process.

The idea behind this book is to mark the current turning point in Hindi cinema, to provide fresh insights for people who know Hindi films well and to introduce this amazing film world to those who know little about it. 'The Indian Cinema Story' is brought alive by the perceptive and varied comments of film directors, music directors, dance directors, lyricists, actors, actresses, screenplay writers, costume designers, playback singers and stuntmen whose eloquent and discerning interviews (from the series *How to Make a Bollywood Movie*) form the heart of this book.

I would like to thank each and every one of these contributors for their openness to my questioning, and for so generously sharing their experiences and understanding of Indian cinema.

This book would not have been possible without the help, advice and suggestions of Ramachandra Guha, P.K. Nair, my sister Shameem Kabir and Connie Haham to whom I will always be deeply indebted. I would like to thank my editor Gillian Christie for being so thorough and efficient and a delight to work with.

I thank my family and friends who have always been a great support to me in all kinds of ways, including Jaya and Amitabh Bachchan, Olivia Bennett, Michael Brennan, Urvashi Butalia, Peter Chappell, Kamla Devy, Damien Doorley, Tara and Gopal Gandhi, Sujata Guha, Saras and Girish Karnad, my aunt Dolly Khan, and cousin Firdaus Ali-Khan, Iqbal Khan, Shaukat Khan, Satti Khanna, David Lascelles, Jon Page, Udayan Patel, Gautam Rajadhyaksha, Mani Ratnam, Niranjana Rao, Yashodhra Roy, Joy Roy and Mrs Manobina Roy. Special thanks to my sister, Priya Kumar, for all her caring and encouragement.

This book is dedicated to the memory of Guru Dutt, whose films have triggered a lifelong obsession.

Chapter One

BOLLYWOOD BASICS

Indian films are unquestionably the most-seen movies in the world. And we're not just talking about the billion-strong audiences in India itself, where 12 million people are said to go to the cinema every day, but of large audiences well beyond the Indian subcontinent and the Diaspora, in such unlikely places as Russia, China, the Middle East, the Far East, Egypt, Turkey and Africa. People from very different cultural and social worlds have a great love for Indian popular cinema, and many have been Hindi film fans for over fifty years.

Indian cinema is world-famous for the staggering amount of films it produces: the number is constantly on the increase, and recent sources estimate that a total output of some 800 films a year are made in different cities including Madras, Bangalore, Calcutta and Hyderabad. Of this astonishing number, those films made in Bombay, in a seamless blend of Hindi and Urdu, have the widest distribution within India and internationally. The two sister languages are spoken in six northern states and understood by over 500 million people on the Indian subcontinent alone – reason enough for Hindi and Urdu to be chosen above the fourteen official Indian languages to become the languages of Indian popular cinema when sound came to the Indian silver screen in 1931.

The Hindi film continues to captivate audiences from Lahore to Lagos. But how does it keep so many millions in its grip? How has it overcome regional differences within India, where linguistic barriers and regional customs differ so much, to become the dominant form of entertainment? One great advantage that Hindi cinema has always enjoyed over the commercial cinemas of other regions is its ability to create a composite world. Divisions of religion and caste, or differences in regional cultures and languages, have always been glossed over in Indian popular cinema. From the 1930s, when sound first featured in Indian movies, the Bombay film was rightfully labelled the 'All India' talkie.

The typical Hindi film has always been a product of cultural pickings aimed to appeal to a pan-Indian audience, and the latest source of inspiration is global culture. It's quite natural that a Hindi film hero is equally acceptable to cinema-goers whether dancing the *bhangra* at a wedding, singing a *qawwali* in a contest to win the heroine's heart, or mirroring Michael Jackson's dancing style with Sydney Harbour Bridge as backdrop. But when it comes to making big decisions, especially that of whom the hero or heroine will marry, the Hindi film always reverts to tradition, demonstrating the respectful return to the status quo that the audience demands. Perhaps Hindi film's insistence on tradition enables cinema audiences to define what it means to be Indian, outlining the values by which an Indian must live. That said, one of the most influential screenwriters in India, Javed Akhtar, who co-wrote many blockbusters in the 1970s, believes that over the years Hindi cinema has developed a stylized form that operates outside the restrictions of reality:

Javed Akhtar: India is a country where there are many cultures, many languages, many sub-cultures, many states. Each have their own identity, their own culture, their own language. Bengalis speak Bengali, they have a different culture, a different ethos. In Gujarat, they have a different culture, a different ethos. In the same way, we have one more culture and one more ethos, and one more state – that of Hindi cinema. Hindi cinema has its own traditions, its own culture and language. It is familiar and recognizable to the rest of India and the rest of India identifies with it. Shall we say that Hindi cinema is our nearest neighbour? And we know our neighbours well and we understand them. In Hindi cinema, a son can tell his mother, *'Ma, mujhe samajhne ki koshish karo'* ('Mother, try to understand me'). Now, in India, no son would ever say such a thing to his mother, that's for sure. We have our own screen fathers, fathers who wear dressing gowns and hold a pipe; a father who decides his daughter can never marry the man she loves. Hindi film audiences understand that culture, they are familiar with it, so they keep seeing the films. Sometimes the audience is critical, sometimes amused, sometimes irritated, but I suppose you can't change your neighbours [*laughs*].

Unlike Hindi cinema, India's New Cinema, which originated in 1969 with Mrinal Sen's *Bhuvan Shome*, was aimed at the educated middle classes. Directors including Shyam Benegal, G. Aravindan, Adoor Gopalakrishan, Girish Kasaravalli, Gautam Ghosh, Buddhadeb Das Gupta and Ketan Mehta made films that were based on a great variety of storytelling traditions and chose subjects that reflected social realities. Unlike most Hindi films, which tend to present a homogenous, and often fantasized, image of India, the New Cinema films made it a point to stress differences in regional cultures, languages and customs. These films were made in regional languages, and the fact that many New Cinema productions were financed by the government, through the National Film Development Corporation, meant that appealing to the box-office wasn't the main objective.

Many New Cinema directors rejected the use of song and dance in their narratives, and their films dealt with themes such as caste, oppressive landlords, political corruption and the exploitation of workers and women – a far cry from Indian popular cinema's preoccupation with romance. Another important contrast between the popular and the art cinema was evident in the approach to acting styles. Director Shyam Benegal, for example, introduced many talented actors to the screen, including Shabana Azmi, Smita Patil, Naseeruddin Shah and Om Puri. In contrast to the glamorous and theatrical styles largely prevalent in Hindi popular cinema, the New Cinema actors, as with Western equivalents such as Robert De Niro or Dustin Hoffman, brought realism and naturalism to their performances.

The Indian director most famous in the West is undoubtedly Satyajit Ray. From his first film, the unforgettable *Pather Panchali* (1955), Ray has been regarded as working in a category of his own, as is his contemporary, the brilliant Ritwik Ghatak. Ghatak's films, including *Meghe Dhaka Tara* (1960) and *Subarnarekha* (1965), have brought Bengali cinema international acclaim. Satyajit Ray and Ritwik Ghatak have clearly influenced many New Cinema directors in the way they later developed their school of filmmaking. But often the success of these films has been limited to regional cities, film festivals, Indian and European television, whereas the idea behind Indian commercial cinema has always been to rely on formulaic entertainment to reach the greatest number. Celebrated screenwriter, director and actor Girish Karnad has been an essential contributor to the New Cinema movement in both north and south India, and has written and acted in Shyam Benegal's best films:

Girish Karnad: You have two cinema traditions in India – one is the popular film and the other, the art film, which flowers out in Satyajit Ray, and continues in Mrinal Sen, Shyam Benegal and my kind of film. Ghatak was Ray's contemporary and was a great filmmaker. You can't say he was influenced by Ray, but he was a product of the same thing. But Ghatak never got the recognition that he deserved. The kind of films that we attempted to make were the art films. They remained pure, they didn't have songs, and in those days, if you sold your film in London or Berlin, it covered your costs.

In the 1970s, there was also the parallel cinema, with directors like Hrishikesh Mukherjee and Basu Chatterji and Gulzar and later, Sai Paranjpye. Their films had songs and dances and sentiment and appealed to the middle class. By the 1980s, all the art cinema directors were making serials for television. The middle classes wouldn't step out of the house. The cities had become so overcrowded and lawless that the middle classes, even if they had a car and driver, would prefer to see something on television rather than go out. The art cinema was finished by the 1980s because there was no audience.

In the early 1990s, from one state-run television channel, Doordarshan, an incredible growth of cable, satellite and television channels had mushroomed in Asia. Many of these belonged to Rupert Murdoch, and were beamed in from Hong Kong. At first, Indian film producers feared that the popularity of Hindi films would decrease because of the new multi-channel competition, but they soon realized that television gave their films an even greater reach, not only in India but throughout Asia. Half-hour programmes showing film songs, star interviews and the movies themselves have become the mainstay of television programming. Hindi cinema has never enjoyed as much influence as it has today; it is at the heart of popular culture in Indian big cities, influencing music, fashion and the world of entertainment. In fact, the appeal and success of Bollywood movies has become a worldwide phenomenon, and in Britain, they now regularly enter the box-office charts as never before.

In India, however, there seems to be a greater divide between city and rural audiences, as the changing values and modern heroes depicted on the screen do not reflect the social reality that exists across the country. Director Karan Johar, whose first film *Kuch Kuch Hota Hai* became one of the biggest hits of the

1990s, explains how an Indian audience reacts differently to a film's plot, and its morals, depending on where they live:

> **Karan Johar**: In India, we break up our business into 'A', 'B' and 'C' class centres. 'A' class are the cities, 'B' are slightly smaller towns and 'C' centres are villages and rural areas. In a village, a woman is a wife, a woman is a mother, a woman is a sister, but a woman as a friend? No way. That's their belief, and that's how they've been raised; they haven't been educated, so they don't understand a concept like that. So the business that my film, *Kuch Kuch Hota Hai*, did in 'C' class centres was much less than everywhere else. We are restricted as Indian filmmakers. If I try to do something completely unusual, I know it won't be understood. We have to cater for the Indian yuppie in New York and the man in rural Bihar. I always say the most difficult thing to do is to make a universally commercial Indian film.

Any Bollywood film juggles several genres and themes at the same time. Audiences are used to the sometimes extreme shifts in tone and mood. A violent action scene can quite seamlessly be followed by a dialogue in which a mother tells her son never to be dishonest, and this exchange can then be followed by a comic scene led by one of the film's secondary characters. It is precisely this mix of genres that makes the Bollywood film unique. The multi-genre film was known in the 1970s and 80s as the 'masala' film – the term comes from the idea that, like a curry cooked with different spices, or *masala*, the Hindi film offers a variety of flavours.

However, this mixing and matching hasn't always been the norm. Early Hindi cinema in the 1920s was founded on specific genres, such as the mythological or the devotional film. The sum and substance of the mythological theme is the fight between good and evil, and the importance of sacrifice in the name of truth. The retelling of stories known through an oral tradition was an important element in the success of the mythological film; the *Ram Leela* (a celebration and re-enactment of the exploits and adventures of Ram) and the *Ras Leela* (episodes from Krishna's life) are said to be of particular influence in Indian cinema. Such reconfirmation has always been an element of Indian culture – for instance, the endless ways in which the plots and themes of India's epics, particularly the *Mahabharat* and the *Ramayan*, are recycled for a variety of different narrative purposes. As Arundhati Roy says in her novel, *The God of Small Things*, 'The Great Stories are the ones you have heard and want to hear again. The ones you can enter anywhere and inhabit comfortably.' Roy was speaking of the Kathakali dance form, but the argument holds good for cinema too.

In the 1930s, when sound came to the Indian screen with *Alam Ara* (1931, *The Light of the World*), the all-singing, all-dancing film became hugely popular. This genre evolved out of the Urdu Parsee Theatre, a narrative form that had already skilfully dramatized Victorian plays and Persian love legends. The courtly love stories of the Urdu Parsee Theatre are probably the reason behind Indian cinema's dependence on romantic themes and the way they link love, obstacles and tragedy. Another popular genre of this period was the historical film, based on stories of real characters or legendary heroes. The importance of the historical film lay in its patriotic undertones. The grandeur of pre-Raj India, the splendid costumes, the etiquette of the nobility and high drama were a direct invitation for national self-esteem and the will to be independent. Of course, India did not need to be independent to produce films: thousands of miles of celluloid had run through the projector gate before the British finally packed their bags in 1947. Despite having first blossomed under a political power so alien to its own conventions, Indian cinema's thematic and aesthetic development seems to have remained largely free of direct concern with colonial rule. Individual film directors were deeply concerned by the independence movement led by the Congress Party, and demonstrated their allegiance to the concept of a free India in films such as *Sikandar* (1941) and *Shaheed* (1948). In the 1940s and 1950s, a small number of patriotic films and a handful of songs with a clear message of Indian nationalism were produced – the most famous is '*Door Hato O Duniyavalo, Hindustan hamara hai*' ('Go away, you invaders! India is ours') in the 1943 film *Kismet* – but by and large, the patriotic film isn't a genre that is hugely popular today. Hindi films have never been overtly political, unlike African or Algerian cinema, the classics of which are clear indictments of French colonial rule.

The creation of the major studios in Madras, Calcutta, Lahore, Bombay and Pune in the 1930s was a crucial move in the development of a proficient Indian film industry. Studio owners including Himanshu Rai and Devika Rani, V. Shantaram, V. Damle and S. Fatehlal set the tone of film production, playing an essential role in promoting national integration. People of all castes, religions, regions, sects and social classes worked together in the various studios. Film production has always prided itself in the way it has been inclusive and continues to be a shining example of communal (i.e. inter-religious) harmony and tolerance. Hindus and Muslims work together, and promoting national integration and communal harmony has always been a favourite theme of the Bombay film.

The studios, including Bombay Talkies, the New Theatres in Calcutta, Prabhat Film Company and Gemini and Vauhini in Madras, were also responsible for broadening the choice of screen subjects, with music as a primary ingredient. Like the great Hollywood studios, they experimented with different stories and themes while each developing their own brand of filmmaking. The key films of this period show the origins of themes and subjects that have recurred over subsequent decades of filmmaking. For example, the New Theatre's films, particularly the 1935 classic *Devdas* by actor/director P.C. Barua, made in both Hindi and Bengali versions, gave Hindi cinema its most recurrent theme: the love triangle. *Devdas* is an adaptation of Sarat Chandra Chatterji's Bengali novel of the same name. This film also gave Hindi cinema its most enduring male character: the tragic romantic hero. Devdas is a high-caste Brahmin who cannot marry the love of his life, Parvati, his neighbour's daughter, because she is of a lower caste. He later befriends Chandramukhi, a prostitute who gives up her profession and turns to spirituality. In a downward spiral of self-destruction, the Hamlet-like Devdas becomes an alcoholic and ultimately dies at the gate of Parvati's marital home.

The story of Devdas touched millions of Indians in the 1930s, who felt that his anguish would become their own if they dared marry against parental authority. The most popular versions of the love triangle are modelled on the character of Devdas, a man unable to fight the system and caught between two women, one socially acceptable but unattainable, and the other a prostitute with a heart of gold. This theme returns regularly every decade, either in a direct remake, e.g. Bimal Roy's 1955 *Devdas* (director Sanjay Leela Bhansali is currently making a new version to be released in 2002), or as an important theme, as in Guru Dutt's *Pyaasa* (1957) or Prakash Mehra's *Muqaddar Ka Sikandar* (1978).

V. Shantaram was a co-founder (along with V. Damle, S. Fatehlal and Dhaiber) of the Prabhat Film Company, based in Kohlapur and later Pune. He made many stunt and action films early in his career, favoured socially progressive subjects and dealt with themes considered taboo. The resulting movies became known as the 'social film'. Shantaram's best work included a period drama about the vengeance of women (*Amar Jyoti*, 1936 – the first Indian film to be shown at an International Film Festival, in Venice), the cruel injustices against women brought about by the arranged marriage system (*Duniya Na Mane*, 1937), to the rehabilitation of a prostitute (*Aadmi*, 1937), and the promotion of Hindu-Muslim friendship (*Padosi*, 1941). In 1942, V. Shantaram left Prabhat to start his own production company and studio, Rajkamal Kalamandir, in Bombay. There, he continued to make internationally acclaimed films based on social concerns, including *Dr Kotnis Ki Amar Kahani* (1946) and *Do Aankhen Barah Haath* (1957).

Bombay Talkies also made social films, the most celebrated example of which is Franz Osten's *Achut Kanya* (1936) starring Devika Rani and Ashok Kumar. It was one of the first films to deal with the evils of untouchability. Bombay Talkies made many popular movies, including Gyan Mukerji's aforementioned *Kismet*, a film that introduced another favourite theme in Hindi cinema – the 'lost and found'. Though the lost and found theme can be traced back to mythology in the story of *Shakuntala*, *Kismet* made it popular in cinema.

The lost and found usually involves family members who are separated by a combination of fate and villainy, only to be re-united at the end of the film. In later productions, the lost and found theme has tended to revolve around two brothers being separated in their childhood who grow up on opposite sides of the law. The brothers usually know each other as friends and speak of their friendship as being akin to brotherhood. They have yet to discover their true blood ties, and the audience enjoys the irony of the situation.

An interesting twist on this popular theme occurs in Manmohan Desai's *Amar Akbar Anthony* (1977), in which the director depicts three brothers separated as young children and brought up by members of the three main Indian religions: Hinduism, Islam and Christianity (hence the names Amar, Akbar and Anthony). The film was a massive success and Desai himself made several other films combining the importance of commu-nal harmony with the theme of loss and recovery. In his *Naseeb* (1981), the Amitabh Bachchan hero is called 'John, Jaani, Janardhan' and is proud to be seen as Christian, Muslim and Hindu. As long as the separated family members are played by well-known stars, the audience never seems to tire of the repe-tition of themes. One of the current generation of film directors, Dharmesh Darshan, who made the hugely successful *Raja Hindustani* (1996), talks about the kinds of Hindi film plots that have appealed to him:

Dharmesh Darshan: I saw a lot of old Indian cinema before I became a director, studied a lot of the themes.

Indian cinema's lost and found theme, the triangle romance, the anti-establishment films of the 1970s. What appealed to me most? No, not the lost and found, I was not very enthusiastic about that [*laughs*]. I liked the love triangle films. They have dramatic and emotional conflict. What really appealed to me more, is the question of how a human being fights the system and fights his circumstances and emerges a winner, whether man or woman. We had this classic in the 1950s called *Mother India*, which is about a woman fighting the system, and *Mughal-e-Azam*, in the early 1960s, which was essentially a triangular romance, but this time between the father, the son and a courtesan. Then *Sangam* in 1964, a love triangle between three mature adults. I like any subject that offers conflict and shows how a man resolves this conflict; human beings facing dilemmas. Indian cinema has an abundance of people rising like the phoenix from the ashes.

Financiers who made money during the war years found film-making an easy way of gaining quick returns, and this new method of financing movies ultimately brought about the end of the studio era. The studio owners could not afford to pay high fees for their stars and staff, and so freelancing made a return – a system whereby all film practitioners were employed on a contract-by-contract basis. The studio system was over by the late 1940s, and widespread freelancing, established by the 1950s, set the pattern for film production thereafter.

The 1950s was a glorious time for Hindi cinema. Filmmakers created authored and individual works while sticking strictly within the set conventions of the films. The example of Mahatma Gandhi and Prime Minister Nehru's vision of the newly independent nation was also highly influential throughout the decade, and many excellent Urdu poets and writers worked with filmmakers in the hope of creating a cinema that would be socially meaningful. It is no surprise that the 1950s is regarded today as the finest period in Hindi cinema, and the era has profoundly influenced generations of Indian filmmakers in a way that no other decade has done since.

The best directors of the time, including Mehboob Khan, Bimal Roy, Raj Kapoor and Guru Dutt, brought new depth to established themes. They drew on the wide spectrum of Hindi cinema stories, but brought to them a personal vision. The films of the late 1940s, 1950s and early 1960s were lyrical and powerful, and dealt with themes including the exploitation of the poor by rich landlords (*Do Bigha Zameen*, 1953), the importance of sacrifice and honour (*Mother India*), survival in the big city (*Boot Polish*, 1954), untouchability (*Sujata*, 1959), the changing role of the woman (*Mr and Mrs '55*, 1955), urban vs rural morality (*Shree 420*, 1955), nature versus nurture (*Awaara*, 1951), dilemmas faced by modern Indians (*Andaaz*, 1949), materialism versus spiritualism (*Pyaasa*, 1957) and the importance of destiny (*Chaudhvin Ka Chand, 1960*). These films show a complex and sophisticated mix of characters, plots, ideas and morals.

Unlike the typical Bombay film, which relies on the idea of the multi-genre – the 'total spectacle' – the important filmmakers of this period not only made commercially successful works but also mastered the language of cinema. They understood how performance, photography, editing and, above all, music could be used to create a new aesthetic. It was around this time that Hindi films started to receive regular worldwide distribution, and films such as *Awaara* made Raj Kapoor and his co-star Nargis major celebrities in places as far afield as Russia and China. Mehboob's *Aan* (1952, aka *Mangala, Daughter of India*) and *Mother India* (perhaps the best-known Indian film of all) also won large audiences beyond the Indian subcontinent.

The average Hindi film does not pretend to offer a unique storyline. The gamut of human emotions is universal, even if the codes of behaviour relate specifically to Indian culture. And while a new twist to a familiar Bollywood storyline helps a film to succeed, if the audience is looking for originality, they know it is principally to be found in the score. The song and dance sequences are the most important moments – even more so today. Film music is of such primary importance in today's Bollywood that it more or less determines the box-office fate of most movies. Leading choreographer Farah Khan believes that, 'What is saving Indian cinema from being engulfed by Hollywood is our song and dance routines, because they just can't imitate that.'

Songs from the movies are part of Indian culture and life. Bombay psychotherapist Udayan Patel has an interesting view on the way romance in real life, for example, is associated with the expression of love in a Hindi film song:

Udayan Patel: The impact on the audience is actually quite deep because the images of the film, the characters, the plot, the music, the dance, the way of dressing, all have an impact – not only on the mind, but also on the construction of fantasies. So the meaning of 'Who am I?' in relation to life also comes from films. A man told me that he was in love with a girl he met in the city of Bhopal. He went rowing with this girl on Bhopal lake. He rowed to the middle of the lake, stopped there and burst into a song and then proposed to her. When he told me this I was laughing, but he was deadly serious. He said that was the best way to propose.

Following the most creative and innovative decade in Hindi cinema, formula took centre stage in the 1960s. The multi-genre film – in which romance is followed by comedy, then family drama, then action – became the order of the day. An important move away from the social film can in part be attributed to the fact that colour film labs had opened in Bombay and Madras. Up to the 1960s, the big films made in colour, including *Aan* and *Mother India*, were processed at Technicolor in London, at great expense. Colour photography tended to be reserved for the costume drama and the historical film. When colour processing became available in India, it could be used to bring alive light-hearted romantic movies that had songs and dances shot in a variety of lush locations. The formula film moved away from the socially relevant themes of the glorious black-and-white period, and depended instead on family dramas and love stories. The settings and the costumes became more important than the themes. Actor, comedian and television star Jaaved Jaaferi explains how formula and clichés applied not only to the way in which the plots were developed but also to dialogue:

Jaaved Jaaferi: There are certain elements in Hindi cinema terminology that are called 'compulsory blind'. The term originates from a card game. You have to have a certain amount in the booty to start off the game. In the 1960s film, we also had cliché dialogues, like the young heroine telling the hero 'Main tumhari bachche ki maa banevali hun' ['I'm about to give birth to your child'], and the heroine's scandalized mother would say, 'Le jaa is paap ki gatri ko yahan se' ['Take away this bundle of sin'], and the father would add, 'Aaj se ye ghar ke darwaze tumhare leeye bandh ho chuke hain' ['From today, the doors of this house have been closed to you'].

Another typical scene in the sixties film had the hero and heroine set out with friends on a picnic, singing 'la la la la la'. There's a fork in the road and the friends cycle off one way, and the hero and heroine another. Suddenly it starts raining and they get wet. Out of nowhere, they find a little guhaa [cave]. The next shot shows a clothes line hanging in the middle of the cave, and the heroine's sari is drying. There's a fire burning, lightning flashes and finally they jump into each other's arms and we see entwining feet – and then cut to the next scene. They are dry and the hero is saying 'Humse bahut bari bhul hui hai' ['We have made a dreadful mistake']. The hero, who is a pardesi babu [a man who has appeared from a foreign land, or perhaps only from the city to the village], has come into the girl's life. He then goes away to study for eight years. Of course, no one has ever heard of telephones, so there's not a single call from him for years. Nothing. The pregnant heroine gives birth to her so-called bastard child, who isn't really illegitimate because the hero and heroine have accepted each other as man and wife in front of a statue of God in some remote temple. The hero finally returns and all ends happily.

The key productions in the 1970s represented two extremes: violent action movies built around the character of a disillusioned hero who turns to crime, and light-hearted and highly entertaining films known as 'multi-starrers' (because the films were sold on the large number of big stars in the cast). Looking back, films such as Prakash Mehra's *Zanjeer* (1973), Ramesh Sippy's *Sholay* (1975), Yash Chopra's *Deewaar* (1975) and Manmohan Desai's *Amar Akbar Anthony* overshadow most other productions. As during the 1950s, more serious themes emerged, reflecting a troubled era in Indian political history. Screenwriting team Salim Khan and Javed Akhtar (known as Salim-Javed) created a new kind of anti-hero whom the press dubbed 'the angry young man'. This brooding and rebellious character, personified by Amitabh Bachchan, echoed the frustrations of struggling workers in big cities. At the heart of these social dramas is the bond between the hero and his mother; her trials and tribulations drive him to take revenge on a cruel and unjust society.

One of the most versatile actresses in Indian cinema, Shabana Azmi, who has worked in the New Cinema movement, in mainstream cinema and in many international productions, considers the wider context of the mother-son relationship to understand why it has such power in Hindi films:

Shabana Azmi: This comes from the entire social structure in which the birth of a male child is the only way a mother can get any respect in society. She is not respected if she gives birth to a daughter. This is a very hard-hitting situation in India. Even in this new millennium, there are cases where female foetuses have been aborted because the desire for a male child is so strong. Hindi cinema tends to take its basic material from Indian mythology, which plays a very dominant part in our lives today in terms of what our heroes do and what our duties are. But in real life I find, particularly within urban India and even amongst many rural women, there is a change and recognition of the fact that the girl child is also very important. There is also an attempt to bring up sons in such a way that they learn to respect their wives. We see very little reflection of this in Hindi cinema.

What happens in daily life does not seem to interest Indian audiences, who don't usually look to the cinema for realism. They want family entertainment, full of basic values; something that doesn't offend cultural or religious sentiments. Indeed, after the defiant films of the 1970s, Bombay productions settled back into formula mode: a love story, an action hero, a vamp, a villain and a happy ending. Very few permutations in storylines and themes can be traced through the mainstream cinema of the 1980s, but exceptions include the films of Mahesh Bhatt (*Arth*, 1983) and Shekhar Kapur (*Masoom*, 1983). These directors introduced new twists and the themes of the illegitimate child and adultery to the family drama.

The 1980s weren't a particularly strong time for film music either. The movie that brought back music and young romance was Mansoor Khan's 1988 film *Qayamat Se Qayamat Tak* – a love story along the lines of a modern Romeo and Juliet, showing two young lovers blighted by their feuding families. Lead actor Aamir Khan shot to fame as the teen idol of the late eighties. *Qayamat Se Qayamat Tak* was followed by Sooraj Barjatya's *Maine Pyar Kiya* in 1989, another romantic movie with great music and family values, which brought another cinematic idol to the fore – Salman Khan. A third actor with the same surname – Shahrukh Khan – became the biggest new star of the 1990s. Shahrukh Khan began his career in the theatre and television before he got his big break playing a psychopath in *Baazigar* (1993). He has acted in all of the big hits of the 1990s, including Aditya Chopra's excellent romance, *Dilwale Dulhania Lejayenge* (1995), and Karan Johar's delightful *Kuch Kuch Hota Hai* (1998). Shahrukh Khan believes Bollywood shares its dependence on love stories and simple plot lines with Hollywood:

Shahrukh Khan: The Hindi film is like *Titanic,* everything is told to you. This is going to happen, the ship will hit an iceberg and just in case you don't know it, let me show you at the beginning of the film how it happened. Everything is explained, you don't have to think too hard, just enjoy the moments. Films are very basic and 'talk' like you would to a child. You follow the story, you enjoy it, it's full of emotion and whenever you get a little bogged down, a song will come. A Hindi film is a complete variety entertainment show and you don't have to worry about whether you'll understand the film or not. I've seen *The Matrix* three times and every time I've come out of the cinema, I thought I understood a different story. In Hindi films, everything is nice, crystal clear, simple, straightforward. They are not pretentious. Sometimes I feel it's very difficult to make simple things and I think that's the uniqueness of Indian cinema. It has so much in it, there are songs, dances, emotions and fights and yet the format is very simple. I think that's the winning feature of good Hindi films.

Comparatively recently, the Hindi film industry has become known universally as 'Bollywood' – some people claim a journalist from the popular Indian film magazine *Cineblitz* first coined the term in the 1980s. The Bollywood name has divided critics, filmmakers and stars, many of whom refuse to use it. They believe it sets up Hindi cinema against Hollywood movies in an overly simplified and patronizing way, and blithely implies that conventions that work for Tom Cruise will work equally well for Aamir Khan, or that Kajol could change places with Julia Roberts. But despite such valid protests, the term has become common currency in both India and elsewhere. Most people find it a useful way of identifying Bombay productions, perhaps seeing Bollywood movies as a product of large-scale entertainment much in the same way as Hollywood films are regarded. For many people unfamiliar with India, under-standing the term 'Hindi cinema' is perhaps too much to ask. Does it refer to a language, for instance, or a religion?

The Bollywood label has helped audiences unfamiliar with Indian cinema to get to grips with this massive industry, but unfortunately, it also facilitates the lumping together of Hindi films into one big blob of bad entertainment. Consequently, gems of storytelling and genuine classics struggle to establish their individuality. However much the 'Bollywood' label has divided opinion, it is here to stay.

One might also assume that audiences will simply accept any Hindi film equally. This is quite untrue – producers are well aware that out of the huge number of Indian films made each year, only eight will be box-office hits. Indian audiences are highly discerning. They may like the formula film but they expect a lot from it, including fabulous music, romantic dreams and a code of right and wrong that speaks to the grandmother and the grandson at the same time.

Recent productions have a technical polish that previous colour Hindi films may have lacked. Unlike former generations of filmmakers, who catered to an audience whose main source of entertainment was going to the movies, filmmakers today are aware they are competing with fifty television and satellite chan-nels, not to mention countless titles easily available on video and DVD. Young directors know they have to produce crowd-pleas-ing, glossy films to entice the audience to the cinema, and to stay at the top, they have to know the Bollywood recipe off by heart:

Karan Johar: If you have to name five basic ingredients that your Bollywood film must have, I'd say: glamour, emotion, great interval point, a hard-hitting climax and every kind of entertainment you can put into the film. I think these are the key elements. You have to have the right emotions, a completely glamorous look, great songs, and your interval point has to be fantastic. And everything has to round up very well in your climax. That's what I look for when I start writing. That's what you need for a commercial Hindi film. It should have all these elements. Only then will you make it successful – that's if you are aiming at the market in its entirety.

Hindi cinema's most successful filmmakers have mastered the Bollywood mixture of music, love, family values, comedy, fantasy and a staggeringly adventurous choice of film locations (which increasingly have no relation whatsoever to the narrative). Audiences know that films are not real life, but rather allegories for a perfect world, where troubles and difficulties are all sorted out. It's more than just offering happy endings – the stories are full of hope, showing that good inevitably triumphs: the poor man defeats the exploiter; the rich heroine is ultimately able to marry below her class and continue to enjoy an opulent lifestyle; the faithless husband always returns home to his wife and children; people live modern, westernized lives and still respect traditional Indian values; the hero always vanquishes the villain and the dark side of life is banished forever. The most famous of all Indian film stars, Amitabh Bachchan, sums it all up: 'Hindi films provide poetic justice in just three hours – a feat that none of us can achieve in a lifetime, or in several lifetimes.'

Chapter Two

THE HERO

The definition of a screen hero and the persona of the star who brings him to life are closely linked in popular cinema all around the world. Few can separate Stallone from Rambo, or Rambo from Stallone, and the same rule applies even more strongly in Indian cinema. The tragic hero is forever synonymous with the image of Dilip Kumar, and the romantic hero with Rajesh Khanna. Popular cinema all over the world depends on a young audience, and it is essential for fans to be able to identify with film stars. Today, audiences in India include 500 million people under the age of twenty-five, and if you were to ask a twenty-year-old to name his or her favourite star, the answer would probably begin 'My favourite hero...' as opposed to 'My favourite actor...' Amitabh Bachchan, who has been working in Hindi cinema since 1969 and has acted in almost one hundred films, outlines what is required of a Hindi film hero:

Amitabh Bachchan: I believe leading men in Hindi cinema are indeed modern manifestations of mythical heroes from our two great epics, the *Mahabharat* and the *Ramayan*. They're always invincible and they always win in the end. Leading men, or heroes as we call them, are required to do a bit of everything. A bit of comedy, a bit of action, a bit of singing, a bit of emotion. Almost like having Marlon Brando, John Wayne, Bruce Willis, John Travolta and Gene Kelly all rolled into one.

Indian stars sell countless film, lifestyle and gossip magazines, and are idolised and adored. The adoration a star enjoys can even be transferred from the silver screen to the voting booth. Southern Indian stars M.G. Ramachandran and N.T. Rama Rao enjoyed long film careers playing religious figures and fighters of evil, and both became Chief Ministers in their respective states. Film historian P.K. Nair believes a star who turns politician may win votes, but that alone isn't enough to keep him in power:

P.K. Nair: Even today, audiences consider N.T. Rama Rao to be the most convincing Krishna. His image as Lord Krishna was built over a number of films and over a period of time. Once you have that image in your mind, you associate values attributed to that God with this actor. In the beginning it works, people vote blindly, but problems start if the actor doesn't deliver when he is in power. That is why N.T. Rama Rao finally lost the second or third election, whereas M.G.R. managed to prove his worth. He never disappointed his audience's expectations. His image was of a man who fights against injustice and corrects all wrongs, especially those suffered by the downtrodden and the have-nots. Moreover, whatever the M.G.R. character did on screen was for his mother – and the mother character is associated with the land, therefore, by implication, Tamil Nadu. When M.G.R. was Chief Minister of Tamil Nadu, he never let his people down. Years later, other politicians were still cashing in on his image, including Jayalalitha; she became known because of her association with him. It takes a long time for the image of a hero to be erased from the public's memory.

Since the end of the studio era in the early 1950s, stars, and particularly male stars, have dominated every aspect of the Indian film industry on- and off-screen and more so in recent years. Most producers and directors, no matter how important they are in their own right, are dependent on Bollywood's A-list to get films financed and sold. Once the producer has signed a director, a star and music composer, he then sells the package to distributors and exhibitors in India, and to film exporters who control the world market. Advances received from buyers provide the cash flow for the production of most Hindi films – in fact, this is basically the way films have been produced in India since the 1950s.

How does a producer or director persuade a star to work in a film? Instead of sending the actor a bound copy of the screenplay to read at leisure, the common practice is for the director to do a special reading of the screenplay for the star's benefit. When the actor has heard the outline of the story, and if he likes it and approves of the creative team involved, he'll accept a sign-ing amount. This is an advance payment, a percentage of the star's total fee that can range between 1 to 6 crore of rupees (1 crore is about £160,000), and varies according to how big the star's market value is. Once the signing amount has been paid, the star promises to reserve dates for the shoot and the re-recording of the dialogue.

The vast majority of Indian films are post-synchronized, which means a certain number of days must also be reserved for dubbing. This essential stage of production involves the actor watching his performance on screen and re-recording his dialogues using the pilot track as guide. Many Indian actors and actresses find the dubbing process very useful in giving them a second stab at getting the right level of emotion and drama in their performance. Studio stages in India aren't soundproofed, and controlling exterior sounds when shooting on location is nearly impossible, so dubbing has become the most acceptable way of recording sound. Until the 1950s, the majority of films were filmed at night (when the streets were at their quietest) with synchronous sound and this added to the ease of perform-ance evident in older movies. However, dubbing inevitably rein-forces a sense of artificiality and makes it difficult to create atmosphere through a sense of sound perspective. As a result, Bollywood movies have a distinctly unreal feeling about them and provide the actors with vocal qualities that most ordinary humans don't have. Boosting the echo effect to a melodramatic line of dialogue makes the star look and sound larger than life.

Amitabh Bachchan: I've rarely worked on a project which had synchronous sound, though there have been some scenes in some of my films which I have refused to dub purely because I have felt unable to recreate the original and haven't even wanted to attempt dubbing it. Invariably, those moments have been the ones that I have found to be powerful, good, and appreciated, in films like *Deewaar, Sharabi, Satte Pe Satta* and *Amar Akbar Anthony*.

One of problems that we actors in India face is that there's far too much noise on the sets, and we aren't able to control that sound. We do not have the more sophisticated cameras which run silently, nor do we have soundproof studios. The remark that you often hear on set is, 'We'll fix this in the dubbing.' But when we are dubbing, it's an altogether different atmosphere, and it's a difficult job to recreate that moment. Emotional scenes in particular are very difficult – it's tough bringing out emotion and then having to repeat it as though it was a Xerox copy. It's unfair to the artist, I feel, but it is a technical requirement and I often find myself wanting to make an art out of it, to dub in a manner which sounds like the real thing. So we're giving two performances in one film, one in front of the camera and the other when we dub it.

Indian movie stars can work on several films at the same time, playing one role in the morning and another in the afternoon. Consequently, they find themselves going from one set to another, where a different crew awaits them. Further delays to the shooting schedule are often caused by Bombay's horrendous traffic jams, as the star frequently has to struggle to travel from one end of the city to the other. This method of working results in films with a distinct lack of continuity in lighting and mood – especially prevalent during the 1970s and 1980s. Yet producers continue to accept this situation because, ultimately, it's the star who sells the movie. Sanjay Leela Bhansali, whose wonderful second film *Hum Dil De Chuke Sanam* won nineteen awards when it was released in 1999, has experienced the ups and downs of the star system:

Sanjay Leela Bhansali: When the star hears the story idea, they say, 'It sounds very good, we really like it,' and then they commit filming dates and I work for an entire year to prepare the shooting schedule. But then the actor cancels at the last moment saying, 'I can't do anything about it. I have to work on another film that's nearly finished.' Films nearing completion always end up having priority over all other productions. Where does that leave me? This means I have to tell twenty-five other actors to cancel the dates they've given me. Some actors work in television serials, doing voice-overs for documentaries, and so they lose out on a day's earnings.

Stars often arrive late on set, which means a nine o'clock shift starts around 12.30-1.00pm. We do one shot and then we're breaking for lunch. It's a heavy lunch and everybody has slowed down. So the actual work starts again at around four o'clock. At six o'clock, it's pack-up time. But I will say that when the stars do come to the shoot, they work very hard.

In the Hindi film industry, stars are insecure. If two films don't do well, people say you're a flop, which means your market value has disappeared, and that means nobody wants you. So an actor thinks, 'If I sign ten movies, at least three will do well, if the others don't. But if I only have three new films and none of them does well, what will I do?' That's the star system. It is changing, but I wish it would change faster. People like Aamir Khan and Shahrukh Khan and some others are getting into the discipline of doing one film at a time, finishing it off properly, working in a focused way and that's wonderful. Absolutely wonderful.

Amitabh Bachchan, India's most famous actor, is also known for having introduced a sense of professionalism to the Bombay film industry. Bachchan makes it a point to be punctual, often arriving before his co-stars. His stretch bus (India doesn't have trailers) is parked discreetly at the various locations where he works, and is always noticed by colleagues and fans. Like the flag on Buckingham Palace that tells tourists whether the Queen is in or not, if the brown bus is spotted at any film studio, the buzz goes round that 'Amitji has arrived.' Bombay psychotherapist Udayan Patel explores what it is about the hero that makes him so omnipotent:

Udayan Patel: There are many mythological stories from the *Mahabharat* and the *Ramayan* that come together and are condensed into a hero. The hero is seen as vulnerable but powerful, like the Arjun model. Or you can have a physically powerful hero, like Bhim, or the eternal lover, like Krishna. Or you combine all the characteristics associated with the

Gods or demons into one and then you find the hero and the villain.

The hero must be good-looking, tall, slim, have a voice that arouses sexuality and sensuousness and have a bit of mystery about him. Simultaneously, heroes evoke stories from childhood that concern strength, attention, learning, willingness. The hero is nearly always invincible. He has a way out, he has a method to deal with any situation. These are all the stuff of fantasies. We have a group culture and that begins with the family. The family is distinguished by language, food and customs, we practise rituals that are different from other groups or clans. The Hindi film picks common patterns from this group culture and portrays stereotypical heroes.

Take the classic *Devdas* – he is based on a myth of how suffering gives you salvation and glory. These are the kind of mythological powers you attribute to a character like Devdas, and are tied in with the idea that true love is unattainable. There is an assumption that true love will never be satisfied, it will always be unfulfilled. It's a seesaw between sadism and masochism where sterility is transformed into a virtue. And screen heroes are nearly always virtuous.

Every decade has had its share of actors, some who have made box-office history, including Prithviraj Kapoor, Sohrab Modi, Dharmendra, Raaj Kumar, Dara Singh, Rajendra Kumar, Sunil Dutt, Jeetendra, Sanjeev Kumar, Shashi Kapoor, Mithun Chakravorty, Sunny Deol, Sanjay Dutt, Ajay Devgun, and many others. But it is those actors who have helped to change the definition of a Hindi screen hero that are of interest here. One of the earliest stars of Indian cinema was K.L. Saigal, who made a great impact in his time. The talent of actors such as Motilal (whose parts typically resembled the sophisticated, wry-humoured type of character played by George Sanders) and Balraj Sahni (who was a model for New Cinema actors like Om Puri and Naseeruddin Shah), brought a rare naturalism to the screen that was ahead of its time. But, like the actors of the New Indian Cinema, neither Motilal nor Sahni had a mass following. It was always the big stars who defined the screen hero.

Until the early 1930s, most screen characters were inspired by Hindu mythology, then Persian love stories from a Muslim tradition brought to the screen the pining hero whose goal in life is union with his beloved, but who must overcome many obstacles for this to happen. The main objective is the union of lovers, and if union is impossible in their lifetime, they meet in death. The lovers must be young, and the subtext running through this theme is that love leads you to the ultimate union – a oneness with God. This is in keeping with both Western and Eastern theological thinking – the secular and sacred meet, and mortal love provides a path to divine passion. Romantic heroes may not always have spiritualism as a final goal, but they are the mainstay of mainstream Hindi cinema and are reworked in each era.

Another popular model is the anti-hero, introduced to the Bombay screen in the 1940s through Ashok Kumar's portrayal of Shekhar in Bombay Talkies' *Kismet* (1943, Gyan Mukherjee). Shekhar is a young man estranged from his respectable parents who has unwittingly strayed into the world of crime. By the end of the film, he is saved through love, reunited with his parents and accepted back into the social fold. This kind of hero is psychologically more complex, and may be both hero and villain, depending on the circumstances he finds himself in. The anti-hero, like the introverted tragic figure Devdas, can be seen as a model for the characters developed by the three most influential stars of the 1950s – Raj Kapoor, Dev Anand and Dilip Kumar.

Raj Kapoor and Dev Anand followed in the footsteps of the *Kismet* hero, who finds himself alienated from his family, turns to crime and is ultimately redeemed through love. Dev Anand did not develop the figure of the anti-hero beyond a certain number of films but, significantly, these included two of Guru Dutt's early works, *Baazi* (1951, *A Game of Chance*) and *Jaal* (1952, *The Net*). Guru Dutt, who later acted in his own productions, began his career as assistant to director Gyan Mukherjee. Tony, the Dev Anand character in *Jaal*, is directly connected to the archetypical anti-hero that Amitabh Bachchan portrayed in the 1970s – *Jaal* had a strong impact on Javed Akhtar, the co-writer of many of Bachchan's characters. When Dev Anand became a bigger star, however, he opted for a more romantic, easygoing image of the hero and later turned to directing as well.

The other important anti-hero model of the 1950s is that of Raj in *Awaara* (1951), played by director/producer/actor Raj Kapoor. Raj is a far richer and more complex character than the *Kismet* hero. He lives alone with his mother, played by Leela Chitnis, knowing nothing about her past or the identity of his father. His father actually happens to be well-respected Judge Raghunath, played by Raj Kapoor's real father, Prithviraj Kapoor. Instead, Raj's life is dominated by his mentor, Jagga (K.N. Singh), a notorious criminal and, unsurprisingly, Raj becomes a thief. One of the main issues examined in this extraordinary classic is whether nature or nurture determines character, as emphasized by a repeated line of dialogue: *'Shareefon ki aulad hamesha shareef aur chor daakuon ki aulaad hamesha chor daaku hoti hain'* ('The children of the decent always grow up to be decent, and the children of criminals grow up criminals'). Raj ultimately turns his back on crime, saved by his love for Rita, played by Nargis. Audiences also relished the presence of the real-life father and son in the film, and a number of memorable dialogues between the characters play on the family connection. From *Awaara* through to *Mera Naam Joker* (1970), the heroes Raj Kapoor played, especially in his own productions, are clear extensions of his persona; moreover, Kapoor's screen characters are usually called Raj, Raju or Rajan, further blurring the distinction between art and life. After the massive success of *Awaara*, Raj Kapoor and Nargis became two of the first Indian stars to have an international following.

From Raj Kapoor's first film, *Aag* (1948), his association with actress Nargis became crucial to his work. The logo of Kapoor's production house and studio, R.K. Films, shows Nargis in his arms in a scene from one of his early classics, *Barsaat* (1949). The chemistry between actor and actress made them one of Indian cinema's most popular and enduring romantic couples throughout the 1950s. Other memorable contemporary Indian screen couples include Dev Anand and Nutan, and Dilip Kumar and Madhubala, who won the hearts of millions, as did Amitabh Bachchan and Rekha in the 1970s, and Shahrukh Khan and Kajol in the 1990s.

The third member of this influential trio of 1950s actors is the brilliant Dilip Kumar, tragic hero *par excellence*. Unlike Raj Kapoor and Dev Anand, both of whom attempted a variety of screen roles, Dilip Kumar became famous for consistently play-ing similar characters, especially during the 1950s, specializing in introverted, sensitive, thoughtful Hamlet-like parts. He also played a number of comic roles and even a double role (in *Ram Aur Shyam*, 1967) but, more importantly, he brought about a great change in the conventions of Hindi screen acting by taking it further away from theatrical traditions. Dilip Kumar always seemed to know instinctively how to use the mechanics of cinema – lighting, sound and frame compositions – to enhance his screen performance.

Unlike the actors who came before him, most of whom believed they needed to project their voices as if they were on stage, Dilip Kumar understood how to use the microphone to subtle effect, and by delivering his lines in a soft and intimate tone, he commanded far greater attention from the audience. As a screen actor, he also understood that the close-up could be used to convey internal turmoil through a glance, a look or a turn of the head, instead of melodramatic dialogue (another practice inherited from the theatre). These little details marked a shift in cinematic acting and can be directly traced back to the impact of Dilip Kumar's work in Mehboob's *Andaaz* (1949). Playing the part of an unsuccessful suitor (also called Dilip) in a love triangle involving Nina (Nargis) and Rajan (Raj Kapoor), Dilip Kumar managed to communicate considerable emotion in a single shot. Dilip only tells Nina once that he loves her, when she insists on knowing why he is leaving town. Nina asks, 'Did I do something wrong?' and Dilip replies, *'Galati apse nahin hui, mujhse hui hai... yehi ke main apse mohabat karta hun'* ('You did nothing wrong, I did. Just that I am in love with you'). Broken-hearted, Dilip looks down at the ground, unable to face the rejection in her eyes.

Andaaz is a key film in Hindi cinema and is celebrated for establishing new standards in acting and a modern approach to themes, becoming the model for many films that followed. Dilip Kumar's performances in Bimal Roy's 1955 remake of *Devdas*, K. Asif's *Mughal-e-Azam* (1960), Mehboob's *Amar* (1954) and Nitin Bose's *Gunga Jumna* (1961) clearly show why this brilliant actor entered the psyche of the whole nation and why virtually all actors at the time and since, including Amitabh Bachchan, were influenced by him.

The popularity of the tragic hero and the anti-hero started to dwindle in the early 1960s. A new hero emerged in the form of Raj Kapoor's younger brother Shammi who, in the marvellous *Junglee* (1961, Subodh Mukherji), displayed an abundance of attitude, youthful energy, rebellion and humour. Shammi Kapoor was the original rock 'n' roller of Hindi films – a terrific dancer and a carefree hero who never worried too much about tradition and never needed to resort to violence to get his way. Shammi Kapoor's character appears to have inspired the romantic modern Bollywood heroes as personified by Shahrukh Khan, Salman Khan, Aamir Khan and Hritik Roshan. The essential characteristics of this hero are that he is funny, irreverent, young and dances exceptionally well – talents that Shammi Kapoor displayed in great measure.

With the release of *Aradhana* (1969, Shakti Samanta) came another of the most important hero-figures of the 1960s, played by Rajesh Khanna. Rajesh Khanna was one of the biggest heart-throbs of Hindi cinema, and received hundreds of marriage proposals from his many, many fans, including one written in blood. Rajesh Khanna was romance personified, but his reign and influence were abruptly eclipsed by a new and stronger interpretation of the anti-hero. This 1970s version, brought to life on screen by Amitabh Bachchan, was renamed Vijay ('the victorious one', a name used for seventeen of Bachchan's hero characters). From the first glimpse of this new champion in *Zanjeer* (1973, Prakash Mehra), it was clear that here was a hero no one could mess with. Almost immediately, Bachchan's character was labelled the 'angry young man' (although there's no real link with the 1950s British movement of the same name) and by inhabiting this role, he became the most important star of Indian cinema.

Bachchan's era can be seen as marking out a clear dividing line, and the history of Indian cinema can be assessed in terms of the pre- and post-Bachchan years. Costume designer Akbar Shahpurwalla has spent many years making clothes for Bachchan and other popular actors, including Jeetendra (a star best remembered for wearing all black or all white, including white shoes), and has seen the look of the hero change over the years. One rule that stays much the same is that, in contrast to Hollywood, where clothes are designed around the screen character, sensible and practical clothes for the Indian hero are not appreciated:

Akbar Shahpurwalla: A hero cannot look like an ordinary man. He has to be larger than life and wear clothes that no average person would. In the past, we had Dilip Kumar, Raj Kapoor, Dev Anand, Rajesh Khanna, Amitabh Bachchan, and now we have Shahrukh Khan, Aamir Khan, Salman Khan, Bobby Deol and Hritik Roshan.

Shammi Kapoor was my favourite; he was a man who really made a big impact on the film industry in the 1960s with his flamboyant jackets, shirts, cardigans and sweaters. Raj Kapoor had a vagabond look, drawing on the character he developed in films like *Awaara* and *Shree 420*. Dilip was more classy and always wore comfortable jackets and pleated, baggy trousers; he had a similar look to Cary Grant. Dev Anand always played a youthful character. He wore shirts with stand-up collars, bright coats, bright shirts. Rajesh Khanna tried to be a little Indianized with his *kurtas* and all that. He made a great impression on people too.

People are fascinated by a European look; when a boy is born, you hear people say, 'Oh, he's so fair, he's got such lovely brown eyes.' So that's part of the culture and that's how people thought a new hero should be. Well, all that changed when Amitabh came along. He was dark-skinned, long-legged and tall. When I started designing his clothes, I realized that he shouldn't wear mono-colours. So in *Deewaar*, you'll see him in khaki trousers and a navy blue shirt – and that did the trick.

There was much political unrest in India in the mid-1970s following Mrs Indira Gandhi's Emergency rule. It was only natural that audiences would identify with a hero who took the law in his own hands, who rose above social and class barriers and cut through the layers of bureaucracy that people deal with in daily life. Most people have to live by compromising: compromising their values, their beliefs and their dreams. Writers Salim and Javed brought to the screen a man who never compromised and never allowed circumstances to defeat him; a single-minded warrior who set out to destroy his opponents. Whether as a smuggler, a dock-worker, a coolie, or a police officer, he feared no one. In *Deewaar* (1975), the hero, Vijay, tells the gangster Davaar, whose shoes he polished as a child, *'Davaar Saab, bahut saal pehle aap race khelne jaya karte the aur ek jaga gadi rokke jute polish kiya karte the. Main aaj bhi pheke hue paisen nahi utthaata'* ('Mr Davaar, many years ago, you'd stop your car on the way to the races and have your shoes polished. Even today, I don't pick up money thrown at me'). At the heart of the Bachchan hero was deep frustration and anger against a corrupt and exploitative society. Unusually in Hindi cinema, this hero does not have romance as a priority, and in eight of his films, Bachchan is seen to die at the end rather than walk into the sunset with a sweetheart. Manoj Bajpai, a young actor who has played many complex roles in the 1990s, remembers the impact of seeing *Zanjeer*, the first of the anti-hero films:

Manoj Bajpai: I was born in a village in Bihar and was studying in a nearby town that had only three theatres. My father was interested in films, so he used to take us to the cinema. The film that left a real impression on me and gave me the dream of becoming an actor is *Zanjeer* – because of Mr Amitabh Bachchan. I always found him very convincing and versatile. Mr Sanjeev Kumar used to be another favourite actor of mine. These actors were real and I felt I could touch them. But after *Kaala Patthar* [1979], I began to feel Amitabh Bachchan was the kind of man I could not touch. He suddenly became a very big hero in my eyes. Now, if I see him on set having tea or having lunch, it's a shock for me. I cannot come to terms with the fact that Amitabh Bachchan is a normal human being. He is still

God for me, and I still carry that childhood impression from seeing him as a hero.

In those days, the hero would make his entrance on screen and people used to clap, because they knew that this man was going to make the villain's life hell. That was expected of a hero. If the hero spoke, the audience would listen. When Mr Amitabh Bachchan came into films, there was a lot of unrest. There was a movement against the Congress Party and a movement against Emergency rule. Even a rickshaw-wallah had started reacting to mistreatment, so people recognized their stories in Amitabh Bachchan's anger. They wanted a leader, someone who could destroy anyone.

Not only did Bachchan's films provide a sense of wish fulfilment during the 1970s and 1980s, but everything about his life attracted front-page attention. In 1982, when he lay in an intensive care unit for two months with a further six months in hospital, following an accident during the shooting of a stunt for *Coolie* (1983), thousands gathered each evening outside the Breach Candy hospital where he lay, praying that their idol recover. The Prime Minister of the time, Indira Gandhi, a family friend, visited him in hospital and left saying, 'I pray he lives'. One of his fans ran backwards for over 800 kilometres as a gesture to God to save his favourite hero from death. In 1984, Amitabh made a triumphant entry into politics, standing as an MP for the Congress in Allahabad; his rapid political rise confirmed the adoration people had for him. But some two and a half years later, he resigned, believing himself unsuitably qualified for politics. Around the same time, the Bofors

corruption scandal involving an arms deal erupted, and allega-
tions were made linking Amitabh and his brother Ajitabh to the
scandal because of their close ties to the then Prime Minister,
Rajiv Gandhi. The Bachchan brothers took the press to court in
the UK and Sweden for defamation, winning damages and
formal apologies in both countries.

The bad publicity that followed the actor throughout the
1980s had no effect whatsoever on his success at the box-office,
however. He became a bigger and bigger star, even acting in
double roles in ten films, starting with *Bandhe Haath* in 1973 and
even playing a father and two sons in *Mahaan* (1983), giving his
adoring admirers three Amitabhs for the price of one ticket. In
2000, when Amitabh Bachchan's magic was thought to be finally
waning, he started appearing on television, presenting *Kaun
Banega Crorepati*, the Hindi version of the popular British quiz
show *Who Wants To Be A Millionaire?* on the Indian channel Star
Plus. The phenomenal success of *Kaun Banega Crorepati* is
largely due to Bachchan's wit and charm. He has the ability to
make the contestants and their families instantly feel at ease,
and seems genuinely taken aback at the excitement his voice
generates when a player decides to use a lifeline and phone a
friend. With the success of the programme, perhaps Amitabh is
really playing himself on screen for the first time. The popularity of the show has turned the fortunes of Star Plus around, and
it became the most-watched satellite channel in India.

Bachchan's impeccable Hindi reflects his cultured upbringing. He is the son of the well-known poet nd writer, Harivansh
Rai Bachchan, whose poetry is much-loved, and whose translations of Shakespeare are regarded as exemplary. Amitabh is
married to actress Jaya Bhaduri, and they have a dughter

(Shweta) and a son (Abhishek), who also works in films, where he has done well. Producers and directors believe that he will, in time, develop his own style and confidence.

Amitabh Bachchan's success is not limited to the Indian subcontinent. In a recent BBC on-line poll, he was voted the most popular star of the millennium, with Sir Laurence Olivier taking second place. This no doubt prompted Madame Tussaud's in London to unveil Bachchan's waxwork figure in December 2000 – the only Indian star to be so honoured. Stunt director Ravi Dewan asserts that, for the fans, 'Amitabh is like God, and even today people come from all around India and wait outside his house every Sunday evening. They wait for him to come out of his well-guarded gates and wave to them.'

Screenplay writer Javed Akhtar understands very well why the Bachchan hero has managed to eclipse all those who came before him, and every hero since:

Javed Akhtar: If we look back at the forties, fifties and sixties, the hero was the paragon of positive virtues. A feudal society where the joint family dominates is a strongly patriarchal society in which obedience and acceptance are virtues. You have to obey parental authority, and you have to surrender your ego. If you see this as being submissive, you will feel like a slave. The halo over this submission is sacrifice, and sacrifice becomes a virtue in a society where exploitation is rampant. So you have a hero like Devdas in the 1930s, whose impact lasted into the 1950s.

But gradually, with industrialization and a capitalist system, we emerged from feudal values – and winning became a virtue and the hero changed. So in the 1960s, we see a more positive hero, like Shammi Kapoor. We were optimistic, affluence was around the corner and better things were going to happen in the next month or the next year. But they didn't. And that dream got shattered and created a kind of cynicism and anger. This led to a lack of trust in institutions, in systems, in law and order. And the image of the angry young man was a natural, logical result.

As we have seen, political turbulence provided the climate for the rise of the new anti-hero and the initial success of Amitabh Bachchan as an actor. But Bachchan consciously avoided the threat of becoming permanently typecast. In 1977, with the release of Manmohan Desai's hilarious *Amar Akbar Anthony*, Bachchan revealed a talent for comedy. This amazingly energetic film – based on the lost and found theme, in which three brothers are separated in their childhood only to be reunited years later – was a huge hit. His partnership with director Desai was particularly fruitful, and together they extended the Bachchan persona beyond the anti-hero, giving him an iconic status in films such as *Coolie* and *Mard* (1985). In each of these films, Bachchan's first appearance is dramatically composed – low-angle shots are used to emphasize his powerful physique, and catchy dialogue employed to stress his distinctive voice.

By the end of the 1980s, Bachchan could play any part – anti-hero, romantic hero, warrior, redeemer, tyrant, lover or comic hero. Consequently, secondary characters like the comedian, the hero's traditional sidekick, lost their relevance. The importance of the family dramas with their inclusion of various relatives was also on the way out. The heroine wasn't entirely dwarfed by Bachchan's towering screen persona, but was increasingly relegated to the subplots. In May 1980, India's leading magazine, *India Today*, rightfully labelled Bachchan 'the one-man industry'. But in interviews, the man himself repeatedly plays down his part in the creation of Hindi cinema's definitive hero:

Amitabh Bachchan: I didn't develop these characters at all – they were developed by the writers, the directors, the producers. Particularly by Salim-Javed, who wrote *Zanjeer*, *Deewaar* and *Sholay*, and several of my films. They conceived this character out of a certain desire and need that *they* felt was going to satisfy the man on the street – the man who was going to buy the ticket. They devised this character and caught hold of an actor who could possibly deliver the goods. Fortunately, they found those qualities in me, and fortunately when I delivered the goods, they met with success.

Because this image succeeded, suddenly it was used to define the characteristics of what an angry young man should be: he must be tall, he must be lean, he must look strong, he must have an intense look in his eyes and he must have a good voice. But for argument's sake, if the same character had been 5'2", had a thin voice and an equally thin body and had that image been successful, I'm pretty certain all the angry young men who followed would have been cast accordingly. It's just fate. It so happened that my body, my face and demeanour became identified with this character that

was written by somebody else. I'm not like that character; I'm far removed from him. But because I have to
perform, that's my job, I did it to the best of my ability.
That somehow succeeded – end of story.

By the end of the 1980s, audiences were asking for something
new. Violent action films had put two important elements on the
back-burner – romance and music. Following the release of
Mansoor Khan's *Qayamat Se Qayamat Tak* and Sooraj Barjatya's
Maine Pyar Kiya, music, young love and family values were back
in vogue. In the 1990s, India lived through rapid cultural change
via the opening up of the national economy, the extraordinary
growth of television, cable and satellite channels and the slow
break-up of the extended family in the city.

Javed Akhtar: You see, you can't remain cynical or angry
for a very long time, you get tired of your own emotions.
So I suppose that the anti-hero became a caricature of
itself and then, ultimately, Indians grew tired of that
image. The current generation is rejecting much of the
traditional value system, the traditional social and political stances. But at the moment, by and large, we are
confused. We don't know what is right. We don't know
which direction we have to take. And in this condition of
flux, we are passing our time and waiting for some
messiah to come and show us the right path. And so we
pass our time by making romantic films and creating
romantic images.

Hindi films confirm this trend, and although action and violence are still present in many movies, the biggest cinematic successes of the 1990s were those films that celebrate marriage and family life. The biggest hit since *Sholay* (1975) was Sooraj Barjatya's *Hum Aapke Hain Koun...!* (1994). This film, often referred to as a long wedding video, revels in the concept of a modern India that never strays far from traditional values. Other influential 1990s movies depict affluent Indians for whom romantic choices are everything. These films, including *Dilwale Dulhania Le Jayenge* and *Kuch Kuch Hota Hai*, were back on the trail of the essential Hindi film formula established in the 1960s, based on catchy music, expert dancing, young love, star power and the importance of the family. Director Sanjay Leela Bhansali outlines the latest, defiantly optimistic Bollywood disposition: 'Good human beings went out in the 1970s and 1980s; they're back now. Good fathers, good uncles, and good aunts, good families, good heroes, good heroines and great songs.'

As in the 1950s, when three actors (Raj Kapoor, Dilip Kumar and Dev Anand) ruled the roost, Shahrukh Khan, Salman Khan and Aamir Khan (all unrelated) share the cream of screen roles between them today. These young actors work at a time when heroes must be physically impressive, know how to dance and be youthful and buoyant. Another actor who has enjoyed a fantastically loyal following for years is Govinda, who became famous for signing himself up to literally dozens of films at the same time. He was the second Indian star, after Bachchan, to feature in the BBC's aforementioned on-line poll, being voted number ten among the top stars of the millennium. Govinda's screen image is in sharp contrast to the educated, westernized Romeo of most Bollywood films. The character he plays is usually an innocent villager who comes to the big city to make good. Invariably, the Govinda hero hits the big time and wins the love of a rich and beautiful girl as well. Govinda is a gifted dancer and has fabulous comic timing, a talent that is particularly evident in the films of director David Dhawan. Dhawan and Govinda have made several blockbusters together that appeal to both small-town and big-city audiences, including *Raja Babu* (1994), *Coolie No 1* (1995), *Hero No 1* (1997) and many other films in the 'number one' series.

Anil Kapoor has been a star for many years, and has acted in a variety of roles. In *Virasat* (1997, Priyadarshan), Kapoor's performance, as a young man forced to accept the life his father has chosen for him, gave the actor the chance to demonstrate his genuine talent. He belongs to the Kapoor acting dynasty, and believes that while a Hindi film hero must have many skills, he is above all blessed by divine power:

Anil Kapoor: There are millions of people in the world. More than the talent, more than the luck, a hero has to be blessed. Why does God choose only five or six people to become heroes? I must have done something good in a past life for me to become a hero. A hero on screen has to have strong values. He must have internal strength, be honest and yet vulnerable, innocent and mischievous. Everything about him should be attractive. You have to have a certain kind of sexuality, that's very important in a hero. You know, he can't be insipid and boring in today's cinema. There has to be something in him that people identify with. It's a mix of so many things – especially an Indian hero. [*Smiles*] He has to dance, he has to laugh, he has to make you laugh, he has to cry. He can't have only one characteristic; he has to be an all-rounder.

This new romantic hero, the all-rounder, has the cash registers ringing both in big cities and the Diaspora. He is a suitable boy with sex appeal and personality; a man who will offer his woman a secure middle-class life. Shahrukh Khan's screen persona has gone a long way toward defining this new kind of hero. Although Hindi cinema never strays far from being conventional, Shahrukh Khan believes that only atypical actors, including himself, can be heroes:

Shahrukh Khan: If you see Hindi film actors down the line, most of them have been rather unconventional in terms of what is conventionally considered a hero-type. It may seem strange that I should describe a hero in this way, because I started my career with so many negative roles. The Hindi film hero is not a stereotype, he's a hero-type. He should be the boy-next-door. He should be the kind of person that mothers want to have as a son. He should be the kind of person sisters want to have as a brother, and girls want to have as a boyfriend. He should be tall, good-looking, and have the right kind of physique. He can dance, ride a horse, do a fight sequence and romance around trees. But mostly what people tell me is that he should be the kind of person whom mothers and grandmothers like. As heroes, we have to do much more than any other actor in the world. It's not that we're doing a Jim Carrey kind of a film or

a Robert de Niro kind of a film; we're doing all kinds of
film in one.

Shahrukh Khan is an unlikely hero-type and an outsider to the
world of Bollywood. His family lived in Delhi, but when his
parents died, he moved to Bombay with his wife, Gauri. Many
would-be stars find that marriage can be a distinct hindrance to
their success in films; married men don't usually make
successful teenage idols. Shahrukh Khan worked in television
before the big screen, another factor that isn't recommended for
a newcomer. But Khan's determination and talent enabled him
to navigate such obstacles with ease, and he won his first big
break in the 1993 film *Baazigar*. Khan played a murderous
psychopath in that feature, but it wasn't long before he was cast
as a good guy.

The second of the three Khans is Salman Khan. His father,
Salim Khan, is the famous screenplay writer (who partnered
Javed Akhtar to write hit films in the 1970s), but while being
born into the world of cinema may have helped Salman initially,
it still took him some years to register on Bollywood's A-list. He
finally arrived with the hugely successful *Maine Pyar Kiya*.
Salman Khan's body-building and penchant for showing off as
much of his torso as possible introduced a new kind of sexual,
youthful hero to Indian cinema. Salman Khan has appeared in
many notable films in the 1990s, and brought a freshness to his
role as an Indian recently returned from Italy in the marvellous
Hum Dil De Chuke Sanam.

Aamir Khan is the Khan in the Dilip Kumar mould. His
father, Tahir Hussain, is a well-established film producer, and
his uncle, Nasir Hussain, a famous director who made light-

hearted cinematic gems starring Shammi Kapoor. Aamir Khan grew up believing he would be a tennis player, but ended up working as an assistant director to Nasir Hussain. His decision to become an actor took his family and friends by surprise; they had thought him too shy and introverted to want to appear on the big screen. Aamir Khan began his career in an art film (*Raakh*, [1988, Aditya Bhatacharya]) and in 1989 was cast by his cousin, Mansoor Khan, in *Qayamat Se Qayamat Tak*. The film was a hit, and Aamir Khan became an overnight success. After starring in a series of rather mediocre features, this young actor now makes sure his roles are varied and challenging enough to allow his considerable talent to shine, e.g. his performances in *Rangeela* (1995, Ram Gopal Varma) and Deepa Mehta's *Earth* (2000). He believes the ideal hero should be a combination of realism and flair. Aamir Khan produced his first film (*Lagaan*), released in 2001, and is today constantly in demand.

As in the past, actors playing heroes still have to be charismatic and handsome to please the cinema crowds. In their heroism, however, they must reflect a greater sense of reality than the larger-than-life heroes of yesteryear. Karan Johar is among a younger generation of directors instrumental in developing the modern film hero. He believes the time has come for Hindi cinema to move away from the mythical hero-type and reflect the man on the street:

> **Karan Johar**: In my first film, *Kuch Kuch Hota Hai*, I made the hero much more real. He could get hurt, he could get bashed up, and he could be the one crying. He could be sensitive and didn't have to be heroic in every respect. In the past, everything was melodramatic; the

tone of every scene and the tone of every character was slightly over the top. But today, we don't react to situations in the same way. In the sixties and seventies, they always had a comedy track that had absolutely no relevance to the main plot of the film. You always had a comedian who was a big star, like Mehmood or Rajendranath; or you had a cabaret item that was dropped in. The dancer Helen came out of nowhere and sang a song that had nothing to do with the film – but she was a great selling point. Today, we don't need all that. The vamp, the villain, the comedian, they don't exist – our heroes and heroines do everything now. Today, your protagonist is also your antagonist, and we have shades of grey in our heroes. I think the Superman concept of the hero is definitely dead.

Chapter Three

THE HEROINE

Actress Shabana Azmi began her career in Shyam Benegal's *Ankur* (1974). She is a social activist and has been outspoken on a number of issues concerning women and the rights of the poor for many years, and is also a member of Lok Sabha (the directly elected parliamentary house of people's representatives). She describes what defines the ideal screen woman:

> **Shabana Azmi:** Today, a Hindi film heroine is typically required to look like a fairy, dance like a dream and never grow older than twenty-three. And you have so many young actresses at the moment who fit this image. But things are changing, we are seeing different kinds of women emerging. There are films that are tackling different subjects and these are not only about romantic love. The last four or five films I've made,

including *Godmother*, in which I play the protagonist, *Mrityudand*, *Fire* and *Saaz* – these roles were offered to me despite the fact that I am over forty. This would have been inconceivable ten years ago. At forty, a woman is assumed to be the mother of a twenty-year-old daughter, and now it's time for the daughter to explore her sexuality. It's inconceivable that a mother would retain her sexuality, so she becomes this sexless creature existing only as a mother, rather than as somebody in her own right. If films showing mature women succeed, then we will have a greater range of roles – roles that are more substantial than [those] currently on offer in mainstream Hindi cinema.

At the time of the earliest Indian films, the codes of what was common practice in other performing arts were applied to cinema. One of the 'conventions' was that women of good repute should not be encouraged to work on the stage or screen – it was considered socially unacceptable for decent women to perform in front of men who were strangers. As a consequence, early Indian movies – despite their mythological and religious content – featured men in women's roles. Audiences were quite accustomed to seeing the same thing in both classical and folk theatre – it was also traditional for men to dress as women and perform raunchy numbers during festivals like Holi. Thus, when a young male cook was cast as the queen in *Raja Harishchandra* (1913), director D.G. Phalke was simply carrying on a well-established tradition.

Even today, male cross-dressing is often employed as a comic device. Sometimes, the hero wears a sari and poses as a woman in order to enter the home of the woman he is trying to seduce. Popular star Govinda used this technique to hilarious effect in David Dhawan's *Raja Babu*. Leading male stars have dressed as women, including Amitabh Bachchan (for the famous '*Mere anganey main*' song in *Lawaaris* [1981]), Shahrukh Khan (seducing a villain in *Duplicate* [2000]) and Aamir Khan (dancing to an elaborate cabaret number in *Baazi* [1995]), and these sequences are used as a big selling point for the movies. It's ironic, therefore, that one of the very first Indian cinema actresses, Phalke's young daughter Mandakini, appeared on screen in a male role. In the early silent film *Kaliya Mardan* (1919), she dresses up as the young Lord Krishna and is seen battling with the demon snake. There are other examples of actresses appearing in the guise of young boys, but it's usually the men dressed as women that get the laughs.

Women were only gradually accepted in the theatre, but movie directors found women willing to act on screen soon after films began to be produced in India. However, a certain social stigma attached itself to these cinematic pioneers. Hindu or Muslim actresses were popularly thought not to have come from 'good and decent' families, while Christian or Jewish actresses who took parts in films were seen as being above such social criticism because of their religion. Interestingly, the first film actresses took on Hindu names – famous star Ruby Meyers, for instance, who was Jewish, became known as Sulochana. Soon, other women began to work in films, including Gohar, who was known as 'Glorious Gohar' because of the style and elegance she brought to her roles, both in mythological and social films and, in the late 1920s, Muslim actress Zubeida. Zubeida later starred in India's first sound film, *Alam Ara* (1931), a fantasy based on

Joseph David's popular Parsee Theatre play. Born into a noble family, Zubeida was the daughter of Fatima Begum, India's first female director, who made *Bulbul-e-Paristan* in 1928.

Like the hero, the definition of the early heroine was closely associated with mythological characters – the virtuous Sati Savitri was seen as the perfect model, rather than the more assertive women modelled on Hollywood actresses like Theda Bara and Pearl White. Savitri is famous in mythology for bringing back her husband, Satyavan, from the clutches of Yam, the God of Death, through her devotion. Sati Savriti was seen as the yardstick by which all pure heroines would be measured. Heroines were nearly always seen as paragons of virtue, and often as weepy, helpless characters whose social identity was entirely dependent on their relation to a man – be it father, brother or future husband. If she was unmarried, the heroine was always assumed to be a virgin, and if she was married, she was seen as the ultimate upholder of values, a self-sacrificing, dutiful wife. In the silent era there were lots of stunt films, action films and social films that didn't have a mythological theme; but many of these early works no longer exist. Their titles tell another story – of how the Indian heroine was perceived in the silent era beyond the mythological model: *A Woman's Vengeance* (1930), *An Ideal Woman* (1930), *Cinema Girl* (1930) and *Beware of Women* (1929).

In the thirties, women of good repute began to work in films, braving the social stigma. This trend was started by a few educated and sophisticated upper-class women, including Devika Rani (who founded the Bombay Talkies studio with her husband Himanshu Rai), Durga Khote and, later, Leela Chitnis. Devika Rani and Durga Khote specialized in movies in which women are seen in pivotal roles, playing heroines who challenge conservative ideas of their needs and demands. Durga Khote plays Queen Saudamani in the remarkable *Amar Jyoti* (1936, V. Shantaram), battling against patriarchal laws and customs. Shantaram's films of this period are particularly bold and progressive in their portrayal of women. His film *Aadmi* features another example of a strong and fiery woman.

Devika Rani, known for her many appearances in the role of a beautiful village girl, challenged the perception of a heroine in another important film, *Achhut Kanya* (1936). This famous classic tells the story of a young girl (Rani) who is of a low caste and who falls in love with a Brahmin (1940s star Ashok Kumar, in only his second role). The film ends tragically, with the girl sacrificing her life to save her lover, but in every scene it is she who displays the greatest strength of character. Another important actress in early Indian cinema was Shobhana Samarth, celebrated for her roles in mythological films. Like the Kapoor dynasty, Shobhana Samarth began three generations of talent, including her daughters, Nutan and Tanuja; her nieces, 1950s actress Nalini Jaywant and Alakananda Samarth, a fine stage and New Cinema actress; and her granddaughter, Kajol, who is one of Bollywood's most gifted stars today.

Other 1930s films show women not as victims, but as strong-minded people determined to change the status quo. *Duniya Na Mane* (1937, V. Shantaram) is an excellent example of a movie that portrays the world from a woman's point of view. It shows the outrage of Nirmala, a young woman (played by the brilliant Shanta Apte), who is married against her will to an old widower (Keshavrao Date). Nirmala refuses to have anything to do with her husband, and rebels with the help of her husband's educated and progressive daughter from a first marriage (played by Shakuntala Paranjpye, whose daughter, Sai Paranjpye, is one of the few women directors working in Indian cinema). The old man finally realizes the folly of marrying a woman half his age (divorce simply wasn't an option in those days), and commits suicide. Through his death, he frees his young wife. In an Indian context, however, this was something of a short-term solution, because it was impossible for widows to remarry.

Parvati, the heroine of *Devdas*, was another important role model in the cinema of the 1930s. The first version of *Devdas* was made in 1935 by P.C. Barua, who directed and starred as Devdas in the Bengali version; the Hindi version of the film was photographed by Bimal Roy and starred K.L. Saigal in the lead role. On the surface, Parvati, also known as Paro, appears to be the perfect pure heroine. In fact, she is completely unconventional and is prepared to run away with Devdas rather than to lose him. Parvati comes to him one night and asks him to elope with her, knowing that she will be soon be married off to another man. Instead of acting decisively, leaving his parents' home and marrying Parvati, the woman he loves, Devdas asks her, 'Did anyone see you enter?'

Devdas also introduced what became one of Hindi cinema's most enduring characters, in the shape of Chandramukhi, the prostitute with a heart of gold. Chandramukhi is usually the second female lead, and is in many ways more interesting and complex than the main heroine. She lives in the world of men and knows how they think, enabling her to understand the hero better than the woman he loves. The prostitute (or her equivalent in the dancing girl, the courtesan, the vamp and the cabaret dancer) is more of an equal partner to the man than the heroine. She is often seen as the hero's confidante and, in many ways, his saviour. But the Chandramukhis of the world know that they have no way back into respectable society. What lies ahead for them? Death or spirituality. Consequently, this self-sacrificing woman usually dies at the end of the film, or renounces the material world to become a *jogan*, a devotee of the God that she has chosen. Guru Dutt's *Pyaasa* is a rare example of the hero choosing the prostitute over the heroine.

One long-term consequence of the development of Parvati and Chandramukhi is that very early on in Indian cinema, films set up the opposition of two kinds of women: the virtuous, socially acceptable heroine, and the prostitute; a social outcast who later re-emerges as the vamp. These two women are seen to live vastly different lives but, at the simplest level, want nothing for themselves. Their shared objective is winning the hero.

Rani Mukerji is a big name among the young generation of Bollywood stars, and is from a family that has worked in films for three generations. She observes how little the aims of the heroine have changed over the years:

Rani Mukerji: The ultimate goal of the heroine is to get her man in the end. That's the basic idea in all films, right from the 1930s to the year 2001. This may not be shared by the hero but it's the heroine's ultimate goal – to get her man. Whether it is a comedy, a romantic film, an action film, a horror film – you always have romance winning in the end. The Indian audience is not satisfied unless they see the hero and heroine together. They will not like it if one dies, or if the film doesn't end with their marriage, or at least a shot of them being together. Even if the hero is off to prison at the end of the film, he'll tell the heroine he's coming back. That's the basic idea in every Hindi film – the meeting of the hero and heroine.

There were a few heroines whose goal wasn't romance, and the most unusual of these was Nadia, known as Fearless Nadia – and she really was fearless. Born Mary Evans in Perth, Australia, Nadia first worked as an entertainer in Zacko's Russian Circus and Madame Astoria's ballet group, the company that brought her to Asia. After performing for British and Indian troops for a while, she started work at the Wadia Movietone studios as a chorus girl. By 1936, she was the lead heroine in action, stunt and adventure films, a speciality of Wadia Movietone. She later married director Homi Wadia. Nadia died in January 1996. Her stunt movies, including *Hunterwali* (1935) and *Diamond Queen* (1940), were not only big box-office hits, but also delivered a strong patriotic message and encouraged women to fight subservience; in *Diamond Queen*, Nadia declares, 'If India is to be free, then Indian women must also be free.' Her screen character was quite the reverse of the typical long-suffering heroines of the 1930s and 1940s, who were usually submissive daughters or wretched wives left to the mercy of their cruel mothers-in-law. Nadia was also the opposite of the delicate women of epic romances who depended on their lords and masters to make every decision – the only means these beauties had of determining their fate was through charm and guile. Nadia was a powerful female icon, but she was a one-person act. The image of this strong, brave woman who resorts to physical violence to defend herself and fight evil, did not outlast Nadia's career.

Archana Puran Singh, who has been cast in many films over the past decade, believes the depiction of women in Indian cinema is largely an extension of how they are seen in society, and that there are few Nadias living down the street:

Archana Puran Singh: I think Indian films are representative of Indian society, and whatever you see in Hindi films denotes strongly what Indian society is and wants to be. From the beginning of the film to the end of the film, it's full of values. They show a heroine, who is supposed to be a typical Indian woman. Right from the day she is born she wants to get married to one man. So much so that if she gets married and is then widowed, she can never look or think about another man ever again. And after marriage, she wants to have children, lots of children.

Society in India has changed, especially in the cities. You have the upper class, then the middle and the lower class. The upper classes in Hindi films have given up all traditions and norms. And in the movies, rich women, for example, are those without morals. They dress outrageously and go out with other men, and the film is effectively saying, 'This is how the rich live.' So the rich are like villains in many ways.

Anybody independent is questionable. Take the character of the vamp – she is used to pass judgement on sections of society that are not acceptable to the traditional middle class. Films are made for the middle classes and the lower classes. And the middle class always pats itself on the back when they see the vamp: 'Oh see, she's smoking and drinking and she's wearing these skimpy clothes. My daughter doesn't, my daughter-in-law doesn't, my mother-in-law doesn't.' They kind of reaffirm their faith in their own values and they come out of the cinema thinking, 'I must go home and fire my mother or my sister for wearing sleeveless blouses, because the girls who wear sleeveless blouses in films aren't good girls.'

By and large, working in films was still regarded as taboo for women until the 1950s. Actress Nadira (not to be confused with the aforementioned Nadia) rarely works in films now, but she still remembers the opposition that she encountered from her family when she announced that she wanted to appear in movies in the early 1950s. Nadira started her career in Mehboob Khan's first colour film *Aan* (1952), one of the first Indian films to be distributed in Africa, where it became famous under the title *Mangala, Daughter of India* (Mangala is the screen name of *Aan*'s second heroine, Nimmi). In this light-hearted fairy tale, Nadira plays an arrogant and snobbish princess who is won over by the handsome Dilip Kumar.

Nadira: I belong to the Jewish faith, and my parents were very orthodox. My mother was out of a job, she had worked in the Royal Air Force. I went to a party and someone spotted me there, and then I started getting offers to act in films. But my mother said, 'Nothing doing, no films for my daughter.' She said to me, 'How can you work in films? It's not a respectable profession, and which Jewish boy is going to marry you? How will you come to the synagogue?' I said, 'Mummy, for God's sake, will you stop worrying about my marriage right now? Let's worry about our next meal.' I somehow convinced my mother to let me work in films and so I worked with Mr Mehboob Khan. In *Aan*, I drove a Mercedes, I rode a mad horse, I tried to swim, I was hung from a waterfall and I remember my eyelashes got burnt in the fire sequence at the end of the film!

Many women had worked side by side with men during the struggle for freedom in the 1930s and 1940s, and attitudes towards women were slowly changing. The Hindi cinema of the 1950s was blessed with some of the finest actresses – including Nargis, Meena Kumari, Madhubala, Kamini Kaushal, Geeta Bali, Nutan and Waheeda Rahman – who brought new life to cinema. The actresses of the 1950s gave the most enduring and power-ful representations of the heroine, even in stereotypical roles. Urvashi Butalia, a well-known feminist, author and publisher, looks at the impact that past actresses made in their day compared to contemporary stars:

Urvashi Butalia: The older generation of actresses – women like Nargis, Meena Kumari and Madhubala – gave much more to their acting than the actresses of today seem capable of, despite the fact that those women played the traditional roles. They were mothers, they were courtesans; they were the typical heroines, but they brought to the screen a kind of power and strength that left you with a very strong impression of them as individuals, as women. And there is something very positive about that. Those women stay with you. Whereas, if you see a film today, you see young starlets riding on the back of motorcycles, hair flying in the breeze, wearing nice clothes and dancing and singing songs. They are ephemeral. They disappear. I don't remember the names of half of them. But I remember Nargis, Madhubala and Nutan. This isn't true of my experience alone, but of my mother's generation too. They'd happily watch the old films, whereas you can't persuade them to go to the cinema today, because the films have nothing much to say.

One of the greatest actresses of Indian cinema, Nargis, was born in Calcutta on 1 June 1929. Her real name was Fatima, and she was also known as Baby Rani. Nargis's mother, Jaddan Bai, was a well-known actress and director, and a friend of the great Mehboob Khan. He introduced Baby Rani as a heroine opposite Motilal in his film *Taqdeer* (1944). In *The Life and Times of Nargis* (HarperCollins India, 1994), biographer T.J.S. George describes how the young actress was renamed: 'Mehboob believed that stars should have the right kind of name to click with fans and he had a knack of picking such names. He had particular faith in names beginning with 'N', which he considered lucky, so he chose for his new heroine the name of Nargis.' Nargis worked with Mehboob on other films, but in the late 1940s and early 1950s, her image became fused with that of Raj Kapoor. Her off-screen relationship with Kapoor, who was married, was common knowledge and the subject of many gossip magazines. Nargis finally married Sunil Dutt, the young actor who played the role of her son in *Mother India*. Their love story is said to have begun when Sunil Dutt saved Nargis from a fire when they were filming the last dramatic scenes of the film.

In *Awaara*, Nargis plays the young lawyer Rita, a modern, sophisticated woman who is equally at ease both in Western and Indian society. She is the woman who saves the hero from a life of crime. In *Shree 420*, Nargis played Vidya, an honourable and honest teacher who, once again, prevents the hero from turning his back on true values. Nargis has nearly always played extraordinary people, far removed from the image of women as victims so frequently associated with Hindi screen heroines.

The most exemplary heroine of Indian cinema is unquestionably Radha in *Mother India*, played by Nargis. *Mother India* is Mehboob Khan's 1957 remake of his own 1940 film *Aurat* ('Woman'), and is a moving and extraordinary epic. It tells the story of a village girl, Radha, who is married to Shyamu (Raaj Kumar), a farmer. Shyamu loses his arms in an accident and leaves his home in shame at the prospect of not being able to provide for his wife and children. Radha becomes the sole bread-winner, tilling the land with the help of her two young sons, Ramu and Birju (Rajendra Kumar and Sunil Dutt). She braves starvation, floods and storms, while her life is made even more difficult by the cheating, lecherous village money-lender, Sukhilala (Kanhaiyalal), who wants Radha as his mistress. Radha not only says no to him, but in one memorable scene, gives him a sound beating. She is a courageous mother to her sons and ultimately becomes a mother to the entire community. She stops the villagers from abandoning their land following a devastating flood, with a passionate plea delivered as a song: 'O villagers, do not abandon your homes. Mother Earth is calling you with imploring hands. This land and this earth is your mother, you will find no peace, if you turn your back on her.'

Mother India's underlying message is that land gives dignity to the poor, and a woman's dignity lies in her honour. At the end of the film, Radha shoots her son, Birju, who is in the act of kidnapping the moneylender's daughter. Birju taunts his mother with the line 'You can never kill me, ma'; and her reply – 'I can sacrifice a son, but never honour' – neatly sums up this character's unwavering adherence to the highest ideals. Nargis's performance in this film is quite extraordinary, and as an audience, we cannot help but feel her trials to be our own. *Mother India* still attracts huge audiences whenever it is re-released; it is a superbly made film and is one of the best examples of Hindi cinema storytelling. Nargis died of cancer in May 1981 at the age of fifty-two, but will always be remembered as a much-loved screen icon.

Like actors who found themselves cast again and again in the same type of roles, the identity of a heroine and the actress who played her also blended into one. Consequently, many of the great women of the Hindi screen became typecast. The beautiful Meena Kumari (a Muslim whose real name was Mahjabeen), who had a soft and seductive voice, started her career in films at the age of six. Sadly, she died of cirrhosis of the liver at the age of forty, but is today considered an acting legend. Although she was often seen as a suffering, tragic heroine, Meena Kumari brought dignity to her characters and allowed millions of women to identify with their plight. Her best performances came in films such as *Parineeta* (1953, Bimal Roy), *Pakeezah* (1971, Kamaal Amrohi) and Guru Dutt's classic *Sahib Bibi aur Ghulam* (1962, Abrar Alvi). In *Pakeezah*, she brought such depth of feeling to the stereotypical role of the screen courtesan that she became the definition of what that type of character should be.

Meena Kumari also excelled as the traditional, devoted Hindu wife Chhoti Bahu in *Sahib Bibi aur Ghulam*. Chhoti Bahu (meaning 'younger daughter-in-law') is the soul of the narrative, and through her sensitive performance, she communicates the complexity of a middle-class woman who is married into a rich land-owning family. Chhoti Bahu knows that her only identity in that household is as wife (in fact, we never learn her real name) to her uncaring husband. In order to keep him away from the city's brothels, she drinks with him and entertains him as a courtesan would. Bravely for its time, the film suggested that for some women there is little difference between being a dutiful wife and a prostitute. Both women are, through bad luck and circumstances, dependent on philandering men who care little for them. Meena Kumari won her fifth *Filmfare* award as best actress for her portrayal of the melancholic Chhoti Bahu.

The other great heroine of Indian cinema is Nutan. She was born in Bombay on 4 June 1936, and was the eldest child of famous 1940s actress Shobhana Samarth. After spending time at a Swiss boarding school, Nutan made her first film appearance aged eight, in *Nal Damyanti* (1945), directed by her father Kumar Sen Samarth. Her first important role was in *Hamari Beti* (1950 ['Our Daughter']), directed by her mother, and she quickly established her own idiosyncratic screen presence, reminiscent of Audrey Hepburn. Nutan's fine features and the innocence that she seemed to radiate lifted many mainstream romances. Her pairing with Dev Anand resulted in a number of memorable films, including *Paying Guest* (1957) and *Tere Ghar Ke Saamne*

(1963). These features simply ooze charm, and their witty dialogue is ably complemented by fabulous music.

Nutan went on to make a name for herself as one of the first actresses to risk playing unconventional roles, years before the New Cinema movement of the 1970s. She was brilliant as the sad, adopted untouchable girl in Bimal Roy's *Sujata* (1959), and also as a murderess in Roy's *Bandini* (1963). Nutan's acting style was subtle and moving, and she conveyed deep emotions through a lowering of the eyes and an eloquent expression. Like Balraj Sahni, she tended to underplay highly emotive scenes, a refreshing contrast to the majority of Hindi screen acting, which has been rather theatrical. Throughout her career, Nutan has brought a quiet and sensitive dignity to her screen characters. She died of cancer in February 1991 aged only fifty-five, leaving behind a legacy of classic films including *Seema* (1955), *Soorat aur Seerat* (1962) and *Saraswati Chandra* (1968).

Known as the Venus of India, the gorgeous Madhubala (a Muslim actress whose real name was Mumtaz Jehan Begum Dehlavi) was another leading cinematic name in the 1950s, appearing in over seventy films. Her big break came in Kamaal Amrohi's magical ghost story *Mahal* (1949), which she followed with a variety of roles. She became famous as Anarkali, the doomed lover in *Mughal-e-Azam* (1960, K. Asif), cast opposite Dilip Kumar as the Moghul Prince Salim. Their off-screen romance was widely reported and certainly affected the audiences' appreciation of the film's love scenes. Madhubala had a particular talent for comedy, and excelled in classics such as Guru Dutt's *Mr and Mrs 55* and Satyen Bose's *Chalti Ka Naam Gaadi* (1958). She married playback singer/comedian Kishore Kumar, and starred alongside him in several other light-hearted films, including *Half Ticket* (1962) and *Jhumroo* (1961).

Madhubala made many average films memorable simply by her presence. The characters she played hardly redefined the concept of the screen heroine, but she remains without doubt a hugely popular icon and set the standard of beauty in Indian cinema. Many later actresses who were thought to look like Madhubala benefited from this resemblance, including the stunning Madhuri Dixit. In her heyday, Madhubala was considered to be Indian cinema's Marilyn Monroe. Sadly, the similarities in the two actresses' lives didn't end there, and both died young. Madhubala suffered from a heart condition and died in 1969 at just thirty-six years old.

Two other 1950s actresses who did help to change the image of the heroine were Geeta Bali and Waheeda Rahman. Waheeda Rahman's career started in the Telugu film industry before she was discovered by director Guru Dutt and cast in his Hindi production *C.I.D.* (1956, Raj Khosla). She initially became famous for her work in director/actor Guru Dutt's films. Guru Dutt was already married to playback singer Geeta Dutt when he discovered Waheeda Rahman in Hyderabad. Their off-screen romance lasted for about five years, and the end of their relationship undoubtedly influenced the love scenes and sombre tone of Guru Dutt's *Kaagaz Ke Phool* (1959).

Waheeda Rahman's ground-breaking role came as the dancer Rosie in *Guide* (1965). Loosely based on R.K. Narayan's novel of the same name, *Guide* was made by the excellent director Vijay Anand. A most unusual heroine, Rosie leaves her husband for Raju (Dev Anand), a guide who lives in a small town. She does not marry Raju, but instead, with his help, pursues her dream of becoming a dancer. Rosie becomes widely acclaimed for her performances, but gradually comes to realize that Raju is unreliable – he is a gambler and soon ends up in jail. Here, the story shifts to Raju's perspective, following him as he is finally released from prison and finds direction in spirituality. Until *Guide*, few heroines dared to be like Rosie – an adulteress, career-minded and a strong woman all in one.

Waheeda Rahman was said to be nervous about how the film would be accepted, but *Guide* did well, at least in the big cities. Its success was mainly due to the combination of a wonderful soundtrack by S.D. Burman and Waheeda Rahman's fabulous dancing. These distractions helped to diffuse the potentially shocking impact of having a defiant and courageous woman at the heart of the narrative.

The vivacious Geeta Bali was known primarily for her dancing. Born into a Sikh family in Amritsar on 30 November 1930, her real name was Harikirtan Kaur. Aged nine, she danced in a show in Lucknow with her older sister Haridarshan, and was given a job singing on a children's programme on All India Radio. In an interview in *Star Portrait*, Geeta Bali talked about her growing passion for cinema: 'Just as any little girl would dream of being a queen in a fairy tale, I dreamed of becoming a big film star some day. I was fascinated by Debaki Bose's *Vidyapati* and Charlie Chaplin's *Modern Times*' (Harish S. Booch and Karing Doyle, 1962, The Lakhana Book Depot). A collaboration with dancer/director Bhagwan resulted in *Albela* (1951), one of the most popular Hindi films ever. Unfortunately, Geeta Bali's other roles, in films such as *Bawre Nain* (1950), *Baazi* (1951) and *Jaal* (1952), have largely been forgotten. Although she may not have brought radical changes to the portrayal of a screen heroine,

Geeta Bali was an important cinematic influence in another way – she did not look like a typical female star. She was certainly beautiful, but her good looks had a refreshing appeal about them, and her success paved the way for a different kind of actress in Hindi cinema, as exemplified by Jaya Bhaduri, Shabana Azmi and Smita Patil. Jaya Bhaduri introduced a rare naturalism to her performance in the varied roles she played. She married actor Amitabh Bachchan in 1973 and was instrumental in helping him in his early career.

Shabana Azmi: Jaya Bhaduri was an extremely significant break in the mould. She was the one who paved the way for people like me and Smita, Zarina Wahab and Deepti Naval. Jaya was the ideal example of the girl-next-door that we hadn't seen in Indian cinema. You saw glimpses of this character in Nutan and in Meena Kumari in a film like *Parineeta*. But these were only glimpses. In the early 1970s, Jaya made her into a very real person in *Guddi*, which was an extraordinary performance because it had so much zeal and enthusiasm. When Jaya came into films, Rajesh Khanna was riding high and, in fact, Jaya took away a lot of Rajesh Khanna's popularity because people were divided between how much they liked her, and how much they liked him. She and Zeenat Aman have been very important in changing the image of the Indian film heroine.

Zeenat Aman made the 1970s westernized girl much more realistic. She wore clothes that you saw college girls wearing; she wore her hair completely straight and flat, a lot more natural than the hairstyles

of Mumtaz or Saira Banu in the 1960s, who played westernized roles, but always had their hair done up in a
bouffant with different layers. You could tell from the
clothes they were wearing that they were about to
launch into a song. So the look of the Indian woman, the
modern woman, changed with Zeenat Aman, Parveen
Babi and paved the way for people like Tina Munim,
Neelam and a lot of other younger girls.

In the 1960s, actresses were more in demand for their ability to
look glamorous than for their talent. Whereas Meena Kumari
had inherited the title of 'The Tragedy Queen', Saira Banu
became known as 'The Beauty Queen' in the sixties. This trend
continued into the 1970s – Hema Malini, for example, became
known as 'The Dream Girl'. There were many young stars in the
1960s who had great charm and talent, including Saira Banu,
Sadhana, Sharmila Tagore and Asha Parekh, but they were given
safe romantic roles and were not allowed the freedom to provide
a different interpretation of women on-screen.

One actress often forgotten in discussions about the female
icons of Hindi cinema is Vyjayantimala. Like Rekha, Hema Malini
and Sridevi in the 1980s, Vyjayantimala was a woman from south
India who made it to the top in Hindi films. A trained classical
dancer, she worked with the best directors, and her work in
films like *Madhumati* (1958, Bimal Roy), *Gunga Jumna* (Nitin
Bose) and *Sangam* (1964, Raj Kapoor) is exceptional. Like Rekha
or Hema Malini, Vyjayantimala was undoubtedly talented, but
fundamentally her roles did not reflect deep changes in the
screen heroine.

This remains true of nearly all the Bollywood stars through-out the 1980s and 1990s, including Kajol, Karishma Kapoor and Aishwarya Rai. These gifted actresses nearly always play strong and feisty women, but their characters rarely become the true equals of the hero. During the 1980s and early 1990s, a time when the hero took up every inch of the screen, the only two female stars to make any real impact were Sridevi and Madhuri Dixit. They were the only two actresses whose name could sell a film at the box-office. The turning point in both their careers came through association with a musical number. South Indian star Sridevi became known as the 'Hawa Hawaii' girl (a song from *Mr India* [1987]), and Madhuri Dixit was the 'Ek Do Teen' girl from *Tezaab* (1988). Coincidentally, both of these songs were written by lyricist and screenwriter Javed Akhtar.

Javed Akhtar: How do we create a character? We take the morality and aspirations of society and personify them. That becomes a character who is idealized, and then some actor or some actress plays that role and they become big stars. Until the 1960s, we were very clear about the image of this so-called Indian woman. The kind of person she is, what her values and virtues are and what is expected of her. This image was used in films like the 1962 movie *Main Chup Rahoungi*, which means 'I'll keep silent'. With time, that sacrificing, submissive, docile woman went out of vogue.

Filmmakers know that the traditional woman is not the currency today, but they aren't clear what the new woman is. And I don't blame them, because society isn't very clear either. We have yet to develop an image of a modern, contemporary woman. It is emerging, but it hasn't happened so far. And that's why in the last twenty years, you don't see great female characters on the screen besides a few like the heroine of *Arth* or *Godmother*. Sridevi, who remained a very big star for almost ten or fifteen years, and Madhuri Dixit, who became the rage of the nation in the 1990s because of her dancing. Neither of these excellent actresses managed to get one memorable dramatic role. Why not? Because the writers and the directors aren't very clear who the modern woman is.

In films made by younger film directors, you'll see the camerawork or the editing or the sound is much better, or the colour of the costumes and the furniture. But as far as the story is concerned, it has the pretence of modernity but its soul is very old and extremely tradition-bound, and that perhaps reflects our society. The 1990s screen heroine is extremely tradition-bound. She may be wearing a mini-skirt, but the moment she falls in love she starts wearing a sari. This means if you are a good girl, you wear a sari; if you're not a good girl, then you can wear a skirt.

Many 1990s films show women full of spirit, who can be friends with the man of their dreams, or be an equal in the workplace, but by and large, commercial cinema does not give the heroine much of a life beyond her romantic relationship with the hero. Roles of substance have become few and far between. The female character may have developed more layers to her personality over the years, but she is rarely seen as contributing fully to society. Actresses Parveen Babi and Zeenat Aman did a lot to modernize the heroine, but this change was ultimately superficial and effectively limited to a triumph in the wardrobe department.

Since the 1970s, especially in the big cities, scores of educated women have started working, and in some cases, are earning more than their male colleagues. In the cinema, there are a few more female directors and writers. But even women filmmakers such as Tanuja Chandra know how difficult it is to represent the Indian woman in all her complexities and still have the backing of film financiers:

> **Tanuja Chandra**: I'm completely committed to making movies in which the heroine is a very strong character, but for the most part the Hindi film industry has not paid much attention to the heroine. In the 1950s and 1960s, the situation may have been a bit better, but then there was a whole period when the hero was the only important thing, and the heroine became a sort of decoration; someone to sing songs with. For younger filmmakers, women are an important part of their lives. So they try to write characters that have shades – this heroine is single, that heroine is a journalist – but that's about it. In the film industry, they always slip into safe areas. Let us not have a woman who dares too much, let us not have a heroine who tries to step out of the Indian value system. Oh, that's too risky. Let us not have a woman who has sex before marriage because, 'Oh, no, no, the picture will flop.' Everyone is too jittery to try anything new.

Hindi movies only sell depending on who your hero is. In my first film I cast Kajol, who's a top heroine, but until I got Sanjay Dutt, the project was a no-go project. Hindi movie heroines don't represent women as they are in India. There are enough women in cities, mostly in big cities in India, who have realized that financial independence is really important. The growing trend these days, even among traditional housewives, is to put money away in the bank for the education of their daughters, not for the dowry. Changes are happening, as they are bound to happen. But Hindi cinema is the last place to absorb changes. Hindi movies are like dinosaurs, you know, they just stay the same.

Post-1950s, the changes in the Indian screen heroine were superficial and cosmetic. A more meaningful and profound change came from the New Cinema, particularly through the work of actresses such as the gifted Smita Patil (who died tragically young at the age of thirty-one in 1986), and Shabana Azmi. Many New Cinema films, including *Ankur*, *Manthan* (1976), *Bhumika* (1976) and *Umbartha* (1981), show women as they are in India – complete human beings in all their complexity. Smita Patil became a role model for a whole generation of younger women in the 1980s. She worked with the best directors of the New Cinema, and also did well in mainstream movies. Smita Patil and Shabana Azmi believed in the roles they played, and fought to change the image of the heroine.

Shabana Azmi: In retrospect, I do remember the kind of pressure that was put on me when I was considering

Ankur, because it was breaking the conventional mould of the woman; a woman who dares to be an adulteress. I remember quite a lot of people telling me that it would be lethal for me to start an acting career in such a role and that I should not do that film at all. Before *Ankur*, roles for women were divided into two categories. There were the good women, who were usually the suffering types, and the vamps, who were the gangsters' molls. You did not have a heroine who went against norms and remained acceptable to the audience.

So people thought it would be a tricky first film for me to do. But I went ahead because I was convinced that the heroine of *Ankur* does the right thing in her circumstances. And there was something about the entire subject of the film which fascinated me. I am very glad that my first film was *Ankur.* The acting style was a more realistic portrayal, it was underplayed, we did away with make-up and all that. You saw this type of acting in Satyajit Ray's films, but you never saw anything of that kind in Hindi cinema. But I must say, it was the filmmaker Shyam Benegal, who dared to be different. His films have always showed a woman as neither too good nor bad, but a mixture of the two. It made the woman much more realistic, a lot more interesting.

In the 1970s and 1980s, the New Cinema was instrumental in changing the character of the heroine. Shyam Benegal, Ketan Mehta, Govind Nihalani, Mani Kaul and Kumar Shahani have directed countless films that show the world from a woman's point of view. A woman's subjective experience of being regarded as inferior, suffering from casteism, sexual exploitation or domineering families and husbands, is at the heart of many New Cinema narratives. The art cinema heroine may not always break free from her social restrictions, but at least the nature of her suffering is made explicit. When it came to transferring that image onto the Bollywood screen, however, her powers became much diluted. A film such as Shekhar Kapur's *The Bandit Queen* (1994), based on a real-life character, Phoolan Devi, was seen as a bio-epic rather than as providing a new model for the rebellious heroine.

While the heroine of the New Cinema in the 1970s and 1980s was going through many ground-breaking changes, a new woman emerged in mainstream cinema too, for a brief time. She was the avenging heroine loosely modelled on Goddess Kali and Durga, and her main aim was to combat evil in the modern world. She might be a police officer attacking evil rapists (*Zakhmi Aurat*, 1988) or mowing down corrupt politicians (*Pratighaat*, 1987). However, this heroine was but a passing phase; in retrospect, this avenging modern agent of retribution seems to have been simply the equivalent of the popular male action hero, as Shabana Azmi explains: 'We see a lot of leather jeans, leather jackets and images of women with guns in their hands. You had a Rambo, and now you have little Rambolinas spreading anarchy. They aren't looking at all at life from a woman's point of view.'

If any substantial change in the depiction of the heroine has occurred since the 1950s, it has had to be forced on Hindi cinema and has come from outside influences, both artistic and otherwise. Even the handful of women film directors working in India since the 1980s, including Aparna Sen, Sai Paranjpye,

Aruna Raje and Kalpana Lajmi, have had a tough time making box-office hits with their female-oriented subjects. It's clear that the established order will never allow a radical change in the way women are depicted. In fact, popular cinema everywhere in the world has great problems taking risks in its representation of women. If a new kind of woman has emerged on the Indian film screen, she has come out of literature, or the New Cinema, or even the workplace.

In the 1990s, when Indian art films were only occasionally produced, the new image of the heroine was imposed by television through television dramas and soaps. Today, the popularity of series such as *Tara* and *Saans* is forcing the film industry to re-think the way women see their own stories. *Tara* revolves around four women from Chandigarh who move to Bombay to realize their dreams. Tara, the daughter of divorced parents, ends up becoming romantically involved with her boss. The series shocked audiences on many counts by showing women smoking, drinking and using offensive language. In one famous episode, one of the girls was even seen slapping her own father. *Tara* and *Saans* are major hits and educated women now look to television to see a more realistic image of their lives, sure that Bollywood will never represent them faithfully. Contemporary Hindi cinema does not offer the strong, impressive roles that it did when Nargis, Meena Kumari and Madhubala achieved their iconic status. Today's actresses are rarely offered strong roles and have great difficulty making any kind of substantial impact. In the past, actresses were at an advantage if they had trained in classical dancing before entering films, for this was an essential part of their performance. By contrast, many of today's stars come from the world of fashion and the beauty pageant.

Jaya Bachchan: Today, the heroine is more of a model than an actress. She is more conscious about her appearance than her performance. Everyone wants to be like each other, look and act like each other. They're doing Hindi films, but what disturbs me terribly is that their body language is not Indian and this doesn't suit the roles that they play. It doesn't go with the characters that they play. I think most of them remind you of the leading ladies of the late 1960s. The girls had bouffant hairstyles and tight pyjama-kurtas and all that heavy jewellery that had no connection with the role they were playing. Although the heroine of a 1960s film was supposed to be a poor girl, you'd see she had her nails painted and long and she'd wear silver jewellery – and that's supposed to be 'poor'! It's very much the same today. There are very few films in which the actress has a very important role or character to play. The leading lady, the heroine, is just a character actor, a supporting actor to the hero. It's the hero who is doing everything.

Chapter Four

THE VILLAINS AND THE VAMPS

The most efficient way of showing a hero's true courage is to set him up against an evil villain. The greater the hero, the greater his opponent. This pairing of good and evil forces is a well-established pattern in Hindi films; the villain becomes the hero's partner in carrying forward the film's narrative, and provides the reasons for a good old punch-up. The lively and charismatic stunt director Mahendra Varma believes that no matter how many great lines a hero may speak, he is not a hero until he flattens the villain:

> **Mahendra Varma:** Since I first started watching Hindi films, they have followed a tradition. This tradition means that at the end of the film there has to be a fight, and this is the climax of the movie. The public wait for

the end. Until the hero beats the villain to a pulp, the
audience doesn't enjoy the film. At the end of the film,
the public must cheer and leave the cinema satisfied.

The villain isn't only an essential character in action movies. He
also has an important role to play in the love story – the most
recurrent subject of Hindi cinema. The love story usually follows
the Romeo and Juliet pattern: two people meet, they fall in love
and want to marry and live happily ever after. But there are
obstacles aplenty in their path. An outside force (a jilted admirer
of the heroine, or an envious friend of the hero, for example) is
introduced into the plot. This villain stops the lovers from being
together in some devious and dreadful way. And until the hero
vanquishes the villain, the lovers cannot be united. The need to
vary the traumas and obstacles gives the villain myriad ways of
keeping the lovers apart. He can be the land-owning rapist
(*Madhumati*), the hero's scheming cousin (*Virasat*), the heroine's
evil brother (*Aan*), a bandit (*Awaara*) or a lecherous landowner
(*Gunga Jumna*). In the older films, instead of having to contend
with a plotting villain who is always waiting on the sidelines of
the story, the lovers are thwarted by a repressive society in
which, for example, differences in caste keep them apart.
However, since the 1960s, increasing social intermingling, especially in the cities, has resulted in issues of caste difference
more or less disappearing from Hindi cinema. Social obstacles
have more recently taken the form of class differences, exemplified by the theme of rich-girl-falls-in-love-with-poor-boy. In
this scenario, the girl's parents are unwilling to accept that the
penniless, jobless boy is genuinely in love with their daughter,
and see the young hero as nothing but an unscrupulous

gold-digger. In countless films we see the parents of the heroine offering the boy a considerable sum to leave their daughter alone. Such a scenario ends with the hero proving his worth and ultimately winning the approval of the girl's family.

Another popular adversary is the heroine's inflexible father. The actors who play Hindi cinema fathers are known as character actors, and their role often replaces that of the out-and-out villain. An orthodox father may be seen to oppose the hero because of an old enmity involving the two families. Alternatively, his villainy may lie in his assertion of his personal will over his daughter's happiness. His stubbornness is the last bastion in a fast-changing world in which women are increasingly demanding that their needs be met. This 'father as villain' is fundamentally a chauvinist, desperately attempting to deny that his power as a patriarch is failing. Actor Amrish Puri, who prefers to be known as a character actor rather than as a villain, is a master at playing the angry father. His deep, sonorous voice and unblinking eyes have become such a regular feature in this kind of family drama that close-up shots showing the actor glaring at all around him could easily be inserted in any similar film requiring an enraged father to vent his anger on his helpless offspring. The father's expression of horror is usually accompanied by the predictable line, 'I have given my word to my childhood friend that you will marry his son. You cannot disgrace me and taint my honour and my name.' Used in many films since the 1940s, this kind of rhetoric has not lost its bite and still features in the films of the 1990s, including the delightful *Dilwale Dulhania Lejayenge* (Aditya Chopra).

In a cinema that favours formula, typecasting is an essential ingredient. Some actors who started their career as villains, including Vinod Khanna, Shatrughan Sinha, Tamil superstar Rajnikant and even Shahrukh Khan, soon became heroes. But these are exceptions, and actors who start off as villains generally stay that way. Amrish Puri (cast as a priest who practised human sacrifice in Steven Spielberg's *Indiana Jones and the Temple of Doom*) prefers to call villain's parts 'negative roles'. Amrish Puri is an acclaimed stage actor who has excelled in many roles in the New Cinema, working with the best directors of this strand of filmmaking. He has a strong personality and a powerful voice and is appropriately menacing. He has played all kinds of villains, but his portrayal of Mogambo, the deranged terrorist with foreign connections bent on destroying India with his nuclear missiles, in Shekhar Kapur's *Mr India* (1987), particularly caught the audience's imagination. His catchphrase, '*Mogambo khush hua*' ('Mogambo is happy') became hugely popular in India in the 1980s. The Mogambo persona even transferred to the world of advertising, when the catchphrase was used to sell mosquito coils, just as more famous villain Gabbar Singh sold Brittannia's biscuits a decade before by declaring them a special favourite ('*Gabbar Singh ki asli pasand*').

In the early days of cinema, actors who became famous villains included Chandramohan, Shah Nawaz, W.M. Khan, Yakub, Kanhaiyalal, Iftikhar, Anwar Hussain (Nargis's brother) and Jayant (Amjad Khan's father). From the 1940s, the new set of villains were brought alive on screen by K.N. Singh, Premnath, Jeevan and the most famous of them all, Pran. Pran was king of the bad guys in the 1950s and 1960s, and his name became synonymous with evil. In an interview with journalist Madhu Jain, Pran reveals, 'A study was done in North India and showed that nobody named their sons "Pran" during the twenty-five years I was a villain. When I walked the streets, people hurled abuse and threw stones at me' (*India Today*, 30 November 1988). The character's narrow eyes, snarling grin and callous cold-heartedness were all used to create turmoil. Born in 1920, Pran Sikand was a photographer's apprentice, and had no intention of becoming an actor.

A chance meeting in Lahore with screenplay writer Walli Mohammed Walli landed him a role in a highly successful Punjabi movie, *Yamala Jat* (1940, Moti Gidwani). In 1942, in his first Hindi film, *Khandaan*, Pran was cast opposite Noorjehan, the leading singing star of the 1940s. After Partition, the young actor moved from Lahore to make Bombay his home and, starting with *Grahasthi* (1948, S.M. Yusuf), he portrayed the most famous depraved characters of Hindi cinema. He worked with many leading directors including Bimal Roy (*Madhumati*) and Raj Kapoor (*Jis Desh Mein Ganga Behti Hai*, 1960). In Raj Kapoor's *Bobby* (1973), Pran plays Rishi Kapoor's tyrannical father to great effect. It was only in 1967 that Pran began to play a few honourable roles, beginning with that year's *Upkaar* (directed by Manoj Kumar) in which he plays the hero's friend, Malang Baba. In later life, Pran worked in a number of comic and character roles as the good father (*Amar Akbar Anthony*), the big-hearted friend (*Zanjeer*) and the matchmaker (*Kasauti* [1974]). His role as the aggrieved parent in Manmohan Desai's *Amar Akbar Anthony* is a fine example of Pran's talent in comedy as he is cast opposite that other legendary villain, Jeevan. But no matter how impressive Pran has been as the good guy, he will always be remembered as Hindi cinema's most enduring villain.

With the increased popularity of the multi-starrers in the 1970s, a trend started in 1965 with B.R. Chopra's *Waqt*, featuring three heroes and three heroines, an equal number of villains became necessary. In the 1970s and 1980s, many new faces played the villain and one, Prem Chopra, became a real favourite. He was nearly always cast as a rapist and made the villain both slimy and suave, adding English phrases to his threats. Prem Chopra recalls walking down the street and over-hearing people say, 'Hide your wives, Prem Chopra is coming.' He even adapted one of James Bond's catchphrases, introducing himself on screen with, 'My name is Prem, Prem Chopra.' He smoked, drank, drove a flashy car, dressed well and always had a girlfriend waiting for him in one of his *Dr No*-type dens. But no matter how powerful he was, or how sophisticated his methods, at the end of the film, the hero would finish him off in a tedious round of wrestling and punching. Clenching his fist in the air, Rambo Rajkumar, a stunt master from Madras, cries 'Only punches! There has to be a man-to-man fight.'

Another 1970s bad guy was actor Ranjeet, who was well known for his open shirts and his leering eye. Ranjeet came to Bombay in the 1960s, breaking into the film world as the baddie in 1971's *Reshma aur Shera*. Taking on more films than the heroes, he worked double and triple shifts at the height of his popularity. Ranjeet, like other villains, was well paid, but even-tually tired of the repetitious nature of his job. In a recent inter-view (*Man's World*, December 2000), Ranjeet, who now works as a director, reflected on his boredom as one part blended into another: 'You wake up and go to work. You rape someone's daughter, you rob someone blind, you sell the country. How long can you keep doing the same roles?'

Contemporaries of Ranjeet included Shakti Kapur, who was said to have starred in over 250 films, and Kiran Kumar, actor

Jeevan's son, who spent his time on screen wreaking havoc. Sadashiv Amrapurkar, who came from Marathi theatre, introduced two new kinds of ne'er-do-wells: the Gandhi-capped political villain in *Ardh Satya* (1983, Govind Nihalani), and the sadistic eunuch villain in *Sadak* (1991, Mahesh Bhatt). Anupam Kher, who graduated from the National School of Drama in Delhi, also had a brief stint as villain but became more popular as a character actor and comic hero. Paresh Rawal, who started work in Gujarati and Hindi theatre, developed a particularly sinister character with a deeply menacing smile, and Kadar Khan (who also writes screenplays) set himself aside from the pack in that he nearly always brought a certain humour to his villainous acts. In recent years, Govind Namdeo, who has become a top screen villain, has formed the opinion that villains are nothing but bad men based on mythological characters such as Ravan, Duryodhana and Kamsa: 'In the *Ramayan*, we had the ten-headed demon Ravan; now we have other demons, they're all basically men unwanted by society. But they exist and they are the trouble-makers.'

The most unusual screen villain was the smuggler and underworld don of the 1970s, developed by Ajit. Born Hamid Ali Khan into a Muslim Pathan family in Hyderabad, Ajit started his career as male lead in many 1950s films. He soon found himself cast in character roles in such classics as *Naya Daur* (1957, B.R. Chopra) and *Mughal-e-Azam* (1960, K. Asif). In the famous 1973 film *Zanjeer*, Ajit is the menacing Tejaa, and in this role he introduces a new twist to the villain's repertoire. Instead of shouting and hollering, Ajit speaks softly, creating a far more sinister killer. Ajit died in 1998, but is remembered fondly as the Lion of the Hindi screen (pronounced by Ajit himself in Punjabi style:

'the loin'). This talented actor has become a veritable cult figure, attributable partly to his absurd one-liners, which included such gems as 'Robert, give him some Hamlet-poison. From "to be" he'll become "not to be".' Ajit's cultivated drawl as the slick smuggler with his large collection of bathrobes, white suits, gold-rimmed glasses and wacky repartees involving his sexy moll, 'Mona darling', are the subject of a fantastic number of 'Ajit jokes' that circulate widely in newspapers, magazines and on the net, eg:

Mona: Boss, why were you dancing all night with Polly?

Ajit: Mona darling, sometimes I dance with Mona. Sometimes I dance with Polly. Nobody has a monopoly on me.

The 1980s was a great time for villains, who provided the main source of interest in this rather dull period of Hindi films. Indeed, some actors who usually played film heroes were happy to be cast as evil characters during this time, including Raj Babbar, who will always be remembered for his portrayal of the sadistic rapist in *Insaaf ka Tarazu* (1980, B.R. Chopra). Villains in the 1980s were virtually the new heroes and appeared in all kinds of forms, such as underworld dons, gun-runners, terrorists (usually destructive psychopaths who have 'foreign' backing – the identity of the foreign enemy was left ambiguous out of fear of offending neighbouring countries including Pakistan and, at one point, China), evil religious figures, rapists, drug pushers and corrupt politicians. The bad guys were the kings of the action film; the B-grade production *Elaan-e-Jung* (1989) was sold on the basis that it featured 200 fights. Screen villains seemed to have secure futures and each actor developed his own mannerism and style. The debauched landlord as portrayed by Jeevan could be seen in dozens of films, twirling his great moustache and leering at all the passing village belles. Both the city and village villain shared a diabolical laugh and a sequinned jacket, not forgetting snow-white shoes; most Hindi film villains deserved to be immediately arrested by the fashion police for their atrocious dress sense.

Many retired actors who were once famous villains still prefer to be remembered as character actors, believing that the villain's roles were less challenging. This attitude is exactly the opposite of that held by Gulshan Grover, a 1990s screen villain. Grover is proud to call himself 'the Bad Man of Hindi films'. He believes that the villain is as much a star as the hero, and argues that unlike the hero, the bad guy has more shades of grey:

Gulshan Grover: I remember watching movies as a young kid. The villain in those days was nearly always the landlord, the *thakur*, who exploited landless people. The hero used to be the farmer, or a villager and the villain, the landlord or moneylender. In India, we used to have *dacoits*, bandits, riding horses and robbing people. So there was a trend of '*dakku*' [*dacoit*] films. Then we had gold smugglers. Then corrupt politicians and police officers. I have played the role of the villain in more than 250 films. And believe me, I love it, because I am not a reject hero, I'm a villain out of choice. To be a success-ful and effective villain, you need to be multi-talented. You need to have a personality that exudes violence, you need a good voice, and the right body language. And interesting eyes that can frighten people, that can do mean things. The moment I come on screen, there is a major sensation in the theatre. The audience feel, 'Ah, now this movie is going to get hot.' The audience loves the villain because he can do things they can't. He can harass somebody, mistreat a woman, break the rules, drive any old way, ignore traffic lights, and much, much worse. People consider the bad man to be a great entertainer, a talented actor. I make sure I change my look in every film. I use different wigs and accessories. Sometimes I am a fat politician. I've also played a very old man. But the sad thing is that people are not going to remember a villain as a great actor.

When Javed Akhtar and Salim Khan wrote the screenplay for Ramesh Sippy's brilliant film *Sholay*, they did not realize that in the character of Gabbar Singh they were creating a villain who would end up being more popular than the film's valiant heroes. Amjad Khan, who came from the Delhi theatre, was not first choice, but what he brought to the character of Gabbar has subsequently immortalized him. Gabbar Singh is a cross between a Mexican bandit and a ruthless psychopath. He is the most sophisticated villain of Hindi films because he is completely unpredictable and does not follow a clichéd path of evil. This dark character has entered the collective psyche as Indian cinema's most powerful villain. His dialogue includes the famous line, *'Jab bachchaa raat ko rotaa hai to maa kahti hai, betaa so jaa, so jaa nahin to Gabbar Singh aa jaayegaa'* ('When mothers put their crying children to bed, they say, "Sleep, or else Gabbar Singh will come"'). Javed Akhtar, who co-wrote this most memorable and complex of Hindi screen villains, believes that the villain reflects the changing morality better than the hero:

Javed Akhtar: The hero doesn't change much. He remains virtuous, he's nice, he's wonderful, he's upright and a man of principles. But in his counterpoint, the villain, we can identify more obvious changes. In fact, in the character of the Hindi cinema villain, you can trace the socio-political history of the last seventy or eighty years. The hero is always the foil, the destroyer of this evil force; but what is this evil force? In the 1930s, the villain was a *zamindar*, a landlord. In the 1950s, he became the mill-owner, the industrialist, the capitalist. He became the capitalist when we had dreams of socialism. And then, gradually, we accepted capitalism and the smuggler became the villain. A smuggler who upsets the system and is a disturbing element in the capitalistic system. By the 1970s, the smuggler becomes the hero. And lo and behold, the villain becomes the policeman or the politician. And that phase passed with time.

Now, in 2001, we see the image of the hero and the villain is very confused. You can have a clear-cut hero, and a clear-cut villain only if you are clear about your do's and don'ts. What is your virtue? And what is your vice? What is good and what is bad? And at the moment, society is at a crossroads, so we are really confused about our socio-political value systems. By and large, we are confused. We don't know what is right. We don't

know which direction we have to take. And in this condition of flux, we pass our time and wait for some messiah
to come and show us the right path. And we pass our
time in making romantic films and creating romantic
images. That's why both the hero and the villain at the
moment are hiding behind the love story.

Recently, a trend has developed in the Bollywood movie whereby
less of the plot is hung on the villain and more emphasis is
placed on love stories and family dramas. If these reassuring,
light-hearted feel-good movies place obstacles in the way of the
lovers, they are caused by objecting parents, or the cruel hand
of fate that forces the lovers apart. The action film still has a
steady following in small-town India, but in big cities and in the
Diaspora, Indian audiences seem to prefer lighter movies that
offer glamorous locations and dance music. In recent years, the
exciting and violent *Satya* (1999, Ram Gopal Varma) introduced a
variant on the villain in the form of an edgy, silent, mafia-type
resembling the anti-heroes in Martin Scorsese's 1990 epic
GoodFellas. But unusual villains such as Gabbar Singh have not
been characteristic of recent productions. Perhaps this is
because new heroes, including the hottest young star, Hritik
Roshan, are happy to play negative roles. Far from alienating his
mass following, Hritik Roshan won himself more fans as the
terrorist in Vidhu Vinod Chopra's *Mission Kashmir* (2000). The
villain may not be as necessary as he once was, but he knows, if
nothing else, he will appear in at least a few scenes of the movie
and serve as punching bag to show how tough and strong the
hero is. For his part, director Dharmesh Darshan would do away
with the cinematic villains altogether, although not the vamp:

Dharmesh Darshan: The one Hindi film convention that I would like to discard is the character of the villain. [*Laughs*] He's very *passé*, you know. In India, our stories depend on the *Ramayan* – all our stories are somewhere connected to this holy book. In the *Ramayan*, the demon God Ravan kidnaps Sita and takes her away to Lanka. She is ultimately saved by the Lord Ram with the help of his brother, Laxman, and Hanuman, who leads an army of monkeys and wages war against Ravan. So the *Ramayan* has the great hero Ram, the great heroine Sita, and the great villain, Ravan. Ravan has influenced the screen villain, but with time the villain has changed. In real life too. A bad guy may no longer be a person but society as a whole. You could have ecological disturbances, or political unrest or nuclear warfare. Villainy is no longer just caused by a lone man who is responsible for breaking up the family structure. In my movies, I'd like to discard this nonsense called the villain. Not the vamp.

In recent decades, the vamp, who was once a key personality in Hindi movies, has been gradually edged out of the list of stock characters. The change came about in the mid-1970s when actresses Zeenat Aman and Parveen Babi appeared on the screen. They were modern, glamorous girls, who looked like supermodels. These new women were not like the typical vamp, who was portrayed as without family, class and morals; nor were they like the demure and pure heroine. Parveen Babi and Zeenat Aman danced like the vamp, dressed like her, behaved like her and at the same time, were socially acceptable and won the hero at the end of the movie. These beautiful women were an interesting mix, and because they were less extreme characters, they mirrored young women in a more real sense. Zeenat Aman, or 'Zeenie Baby', as she was called, was Dev Anand's discovery. He cast her in his 1971 film *Hare Rama Hare Krishna* as the hero's wayward, pot-smoking, hippie sister, not realizing that this young actress would steal the show from the lead heroine, Mumtaz. Zeenat Aman is said to have started the Indian craze for wearing blue jeans, much to the sorrow of sari manufacturers. Parveen Babi, who was the only Indian movie star to ever feature on a *Time* magazine cover (in July 1976), spoke openly about her private life, admitting to having two lovers. Tanuja Chandra, who is a screenplay writer and one of the few women directors working in Hindi films, says she misses the old-fashioned, stereotypical vamp:

Tanuja Chandra: I used to rather like the vamps in Hindi movies. I used to enjoy them and find them very interesting characters. But I think what's happened is they've been incorporated into the heroine. The same thing has happened to our comedians. There used to be comedy actors like Kesh Mukherjee or Mukri, who had their own roles, but these have been absorbed by the hero. Earlier, a heroine could not be the cabaret dancer, so the cabaret dancer had to necessarily be the vamp. She was a separate character, the one with the Western influence, you know. And she was the one who was going to take the hero down the evil path, whereas the heroine symbolized all kinds of virtues. The heroine today can be forced by her circumstances to become a prostitute. But the hero always saves her before she actually becomes one. What happens is that whenever you have an interesting heroine with negative shades, in Pygmalion style, she is transformed back into the virtuous goddess-like heroine before the end of the film, so that audiences will find her acceptable. The hero and heroine are growing and growing, eating up all the other characters around them like monsters.

In the old days, when the vamp reigned, she represented the antithesis of a typical heroine, who was modelled on the notion of the perfect mother, the sister and wife. A vampish woman nearly always had to be a social outcast; consequently, this character is implausible in films set in close-knit communities. If a negative female character is necessary in a story set in a village, then she will be the nagging and wicked mother-in-law, or an interfering neighbour (whose bad behaviour will, however, never include any form of sexual promiscuity). If she is a young woman, then she will be portrayed as the village tease – not all bad, but with unsociable traits. A good example of this kind of character occurs in *Mother India*, in the shape of the young woman (played by Chanchal, Madhubala's sister) whom Birju kidnaps.

The Hindi cinema vamp has to be a product of the big city. Her many immoral traits included smoking, drinking, dressing skimpily and having no interest at all in marriage and children. Most importantly, the vamp was seen as a sexually free woman who lived openly with the villain. By the fact of her promiscuity, she could sexually excite the audience without upsetting the value system. The male audience would lust after her, guilt-free, as the heroine was naturally out of bounds and seen as somebody's sister, wife and daughter. By contrast, the vamp's primary role was to evoke desire, to be a sex object. She sang all the sexiest songs in the film, moved sensuously through seedy clubs and cared little for social acceptance. Despite the fact that the vamp was nearly always a caricature, she showed many more shades to her personality than the one-dimensional heroine. Female audiences have always had great affection for the vamp, seeing her as more human – unlike the unreal heroine. Archana Puran Singh has been cast as a vamp, a wicked step-mother and a gangster's moll in many movies of the 1990s. She argues that the role of the vamp has become increasingly trivialized over time:

> **Archana Puran Singh**: When the producer comes to me, the kind of briefings he gives are hilarious in retrospect. The producer says, 'Madam, I want to do a film with you and there are three scenes, one rape, and then you'll have four songs and you will die, you will sacrifice your life for the hero and that's it.' And I say, 'What is the story of the film?' He answers, 'The story of the film? Why should I tell you? I've told you your role, right?' They do not tell you the story of the film, the whole script is never narrated to you. If you really want to know, he'll say, 'I'll tell you who the hero is and who the heroine is – now you're impressed?'

In every decade, there have been actresses known for their vampish roles, including Begum Para, Sheila Ramani, Shashikala, Vijayalakshmi and Kuldip Kaur. But the most famous vamp of Hindi cinema is undoubtedly the amazing Helen, who is said to have appeared in a thousand films. She reigned supreme from the late 1950s to the early 1970s, and became a top star, due primarily to her fantastic figure and exceptional dance talent. There was a time that a Helen number had to be included in nearly every Hindi film, whether or not her cabaret performance bore any connection to the narrative. Helen remembers that film distributors believed her dance would bring the film good luck.

Helen Richardson is of Burmese and Spanish origin, and was born in Rangoon in 1940. During the Second World War, her father, who was in the diplomatic corps, went missing, and her mother, Marlene Richardson, fled Burma during the war years with the children. After a gruelling eight months of travel, sometimes by elephant and sometimes on foot, the Richardsons arrived in Calcutta and finally moved to Bombay with virtually no money to speak of.

> **Helen:** I had to leave school because I had to look after my sister and brother. My mother had met Cuckoo, the greatest dancer of those years, and asked her to help me get into the film industry. I was hardly fourteen. I started as a group dancer and was paid thirty-five rupees [equivalent to fifty pence today] for a shift from 9.00am to 6.00pm, or 9.00pm to 6.00am the next morning. I got my big break in *Baarish* in a song titled, '*Mr John, Baba Khan, Lala Roshandaan*'.
>
> The dancer had to be a vamp in those days. The public would take to the vamp because she related to the real world. You know, a woman is not only sugar, she has to be spice too. The heroine was too goody-goody,

wishy-washy for my liking. The vamp had to be seductive, a brazen hussy, have a cigarette in one hand, a glass of whisky in the other. I could never walk on the streets. I had to wear a *burqa* [veil]. They used to go berserk if they saw me. I'd get a lot of fan mail, even from women. I became a sex symbol in the Sixties. I was known as the H-Bomb – H for Helen; that made me laugh a lot!

Helen appeared in outlandish clothes – feather boas, fishnet stockings, elbow-length gloves. Her gorgeous numbers and gorgeous clothes were the highlight of many films, and she often overshadowed the insipid heroine. One of Helen's last memorable dances was performed to entertain the villain of villains, Gabbar Singh, in *Sholay*. In 1981, she became the second wife of screenplay writer Salim Khan and now occasionally appears on screen in the role of a doting mother. But she will always be remembered as the most-loved vamp of Hindi cinema.

A few other actresses made their mark as vamps after Helen, but no one matched her oomph until the superb Bindu arrived on the scene in the 1970s. Bindu subsequently acted in so many vamp roles that she came to know every facet of this character.

Bindu: The vamp is usually a loner. You hardly ever know who her parents are, or what kind of family she is from. If she is seen as having parents, they either hate her or disown her. We assume the vamp is usually from a poor family. But she wants more from life and she cannot tolerate being poor. She's always after money. Everything about her character is bad. She will try and come between the hero and heroine and try and seduce the hero and separate him from his sweetheart. She'll try to steal the hero. If the vamp happens to marry and becomes a bride, she will stir trouble in the marital home by fighting with the in-laws. She will try and persuade her husband to live apart from his family. Sometimes the vamp is a cabaret dancer. She lives in a world that has no connection with good people and good society. She dances to the tune of the villain. She listens to him and cares only for him. In fact, the only friend she has is the villain and they are bound together by self-interest rather than genuine feelings.

Another popular character of Indian cinema is the courtesan (based on the traditional *tawaif*) or the dancing girl (*nautch* girl), who has been a regular in Hindi films since the 1930s. In her article *Transcending the Boundaries of Identity*, Vidya Rao describes how *tawaifs* were different from wives: 'The *tawaifs* who lived and performed about a generation ago appear to be counterpoints to the image of the good wife. At a time when most women received no education, had no economic or political power, the *tawaifs* were wealthy, powerful, intelligent artists.' The *tawaif* had the protection of a patron and was trained in singing and dancing. She was sophisticated and cultured. In the movies, the courtesan or dancing woman becomes a tragic figure.

The most famous example of the ill-fated courtesan occurs in Kamaal Amrohi's *Pakeezah*, starring the beautiful Meena Kumari in a double role. Wth its luxurious settings, beautiful music, lyrical Urdu dialogue, fine performances and intricate

plot, the film has since become a classic. The courtesan Sahibjaan, who is renamed Pakeezah ('the pure one'), is ultimately united with Salim (Raaj Kumar), the man of her dreams, after the plot reveals that they are of the same aristocratic family. In 1981, Muzzaffar Ali directed *Umrao Jaan* starring the beautiful Rekha. This film was based on a real-life early twentieth century character that inspired Mirza Mohammed Hadi Ruswa to write the novel *Umrao Jaan Ada*. Umrao Jaan is a young woman of good family who had been kidnapped as a young child and brought up as a courtesan.

Archana Puran Singh: The difference between a vamp and a courtesan is that the vamp has choices. The courtesan is someone who had no choice in being a courtesan. She may have been kidnapped or forced to do what she is doing. There is always this sad story behind her. Indians are very sympathetic to people who have been dealt a raw deal by fate and destiny, because fate and destiny play a big role in our psyche and philosophy. We think, 'Oh, what could we do, it was God's will.' So the courtesan has no choice; a vamp has choices – therefore, that makes her a vamp. If the courtesan is performing a *mujra* dance, it's not out of her own choice and, amazingly, very often the courtesan remains a virgin, defying all logic. The films show that she has a purity of mind and a purity of body.

What attracts the hero to her is that she still represents something that is forbidden, so the male may watch her dance and she will fall in love with him, but he will never truly reciprocate that love. And very often this forms a triangle: the heroine who the hero loves and for some reason cannot marry, and the dancer. In most Hindi films, the courtesan ends up sacrificing her life for the hero. So, in a film like *Muqqaddar Ka Sikandar*, Raakhee is the heroine, but somehow, Rekha, who plays the courtesan, emerges as the real heroine. Rekha plays the courtesan so beautifully, she's the epitome of all that perfection. Perfect dance movements and perfect face. Rekha was also excellent in *Umrao Jaan*, a film based on the life of a courtesan. In that story, she is the victim of misfortune.

Once Zeenat Aman and Parveen Babi had made their impact by the late 1970s and created the modern heroine, the traditional courtesan or the vamp became far less important. She was transformed into the gangster's moll, but by the late 1980s even this character found she had fewer and fewer scenes. In the new decade, the character hardly makes any difference to the narrative. If a movie today needs a negative female character, she is a scheming family member, or a ruthlessly ambitious work colleague. But these women are not social outsiders in the way that the vamp of earlier films was; they are simply conniving and wicked. Dharmesh Darshan reworked the vamp in his *Raja Hindustani* into a mean and scheming step-mother, played to perfection by Archana Puran Singh.

Dharmesh Darshan: If you study Hindi cinema carefully, the woman projected as the vamp is similar to the Rita Hayworth character. All the elements of Indian cinema, if I'm not mistaken, are old Hollywood: the grandeur, the

emotions, the drama, the melodrama. The closest definition of conventional Indian cinema is conventional old
Hollywood. We have this great vamp, who's so glamorous. Sometimes, you feel she should be the heroine
[*laughs*] – she's fabulous. She's so much more interesting than the goody-goody heroine.

Right: *Alam Ara*, India's first sound film.

Above: *Shri Ram Bhakt Hanuman*, a mythological film about the exploits of Hanuman.

Left: D.G. Phalke, the father of Indian cinema, at work on *Raja Harischandra*.

Right: Mythological films often featured early special effects.

Favourite
romantic
couples:

Dilip Kumar
and
Madhubala

Dev Anand and Nutan

Raj Kapoor and Nargis

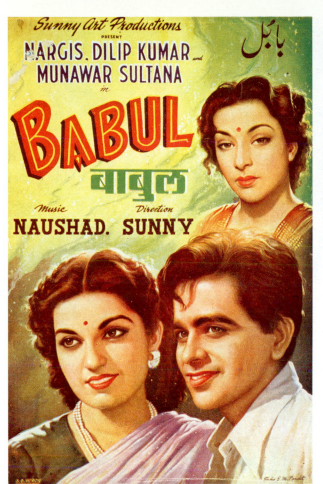

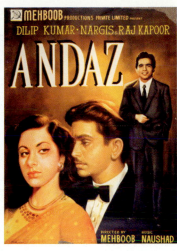

The love triangle has always been a popular theme reworked in classic films.

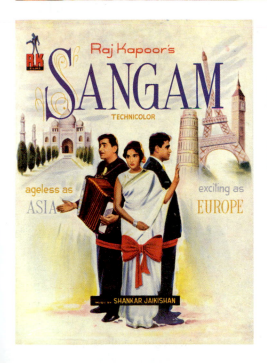

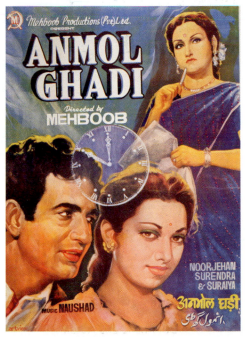

Above: Music director Naushad (left) and singer Mohammed Rafi.

Above: Lata Mangeshkar, the most famous playback singer of all.

Left: Playback singer Kishore Kumar was also a comic actor.

Above: Singer Mukesh working with music director Salil Choudhury.

Right: Acclaimed dancer Helen in *Junglee*.

Left: Actress/ dancer Vyjayantimala with Dev Anand in *Jewel Thief*.

Right: Actress/ dancer Waheeda Rahman in a sequence from *Guide*.

Left: A classic example of the dream sequence, in Raj Kapoor's *Awaara*.

Devdas, Indian cinema's most enduring hero, was
played by K.L. Saigal (left), and later by Dilip Kumar.

Director/actor Guru Dutt in *Pyaasa*.

The first of the anti-heroes:
Ashok Kumar in *Kismet*.

Right: Dharmendra and Amitabh Bachchan in action.

Above: On-and off-screen couple Jaya and Amitabh Bachchan.

Above: Shahrukh Khan and Manisha Koirala in *Dil Se*.

Left: Hritik Roshan and Karishma Kapoor in *Fiza*.

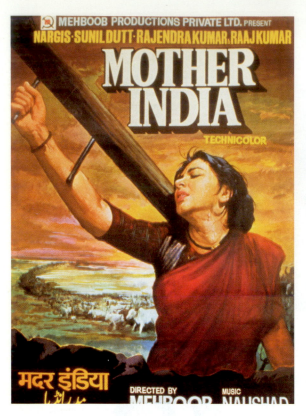

Above right: Actress Meena Kumari.
Right: Waheeda Rahman in *Girlfriend*.

Below: Modern-day actresses Rekha
(left) and Karishma Kapoor in *Zubeida*.

Chapter Five
WORKING WONDERS

Nearly all film practitioners in India acknowledge the strong influence of religion on the cinema of their country. Although film is a Western invention, it was instantly embraced by Indian audiences. But like many things imported from the West, Indian film-goers were only able to relate to these films on a deeper level when Indian filmmakers started to make cinema and its form of storytelling their own. This process began with the man regarded as the father of Indian cinema, D.G. Phalke, who directed, photographed and wrote *Raja Harishchandra* (1913). In the November 1917 issue of *Navyug*, Phalke recalled watching the film *The Life of Christ*, writing: 'While the life of Christ was rolling fast before my physical eyes, I was mentally visualizing the Gods, Shri Krishna, Shri Ramachandra, their Gokul and Ayodhya. I was gripped by a strange spell. I bought another ticket and saw the film again. Could we, the sons of India, ever be able to see Indian images on the screen?' (*Cinema Vision*, January 1980, translated from the Marathi by Narmada Shahane and edited by Parag R. Amladi).

Dhundiraj Govind Phalke, known as Dadasaheb Phalke, came from a family of priests and so had a strongly religious upbringing. He had trained to be a Sanskrit scholar and after his family moved from their home town in Nasik to Bombay, young Phalke joined the J.J. School of Arts in 1885, later studying at Baroda's famous Kalabhavan (now the art department of the University of Baroda). Phalke was put in charge of Kalabhavan's photographic studio and worked on the production of stage dramas, even learning the art of magic. As film historian B.V. Dharap recounts in *The Phalke Saga*, when Phalke was about forty, a friend loaned him money and he went to London. There, he bought a Williamson camera, a printing machine, a perforator and some negative film. On his return to India two weeks later, he shot a short test film, *The Birth of a Pea Plant*, using time lapse photography to show how a pea sprouts into a plant. This footage impressed a financier who expressed himself willing to fund Phalke's dream of making a film – as long as Mrs Phalke's jewellery was used as security.

The next problem Phalke faced was the general lack of female artists willing to work in film, which was widely regarded as a disreputable field at the time; the only women who responded to his advertisement were prostitutes. Phalke settled for a delicate-looking male cook, A. Salunke, to play the role of Queen Taramati in *Raja Harishchandra*. The film was released at the Coronation Theatre in Bombay on 3 May 1913. It had four reels (of which only the first and the last reel have been found) and told the story from the *Mahabharat* of Harishchandra, an ethically minded king who, on the altar of Truth, sacrifices his kingdom, wife and son because of a promise he makes to the Sage Vishwamitra. The Gods, convinced that Harishchandra is the living embodiment of Truth, restore his former glory to him. The story of *Raja Harishchandra* also involves the participation of a group of stock characters, including the comic servant, the manipulative sage and the dutiful wife; set characters who became an integral part of Hindi cinema narrative.

In later years, Phalke made several short films, including a wonderful educational two-reeler called *How Films are Made* (1917), in which he himself featured. Over twenty years, Phalke made over ninety films, from shorts and documentaries to mythologicals and socials. By 1934, however, he had fallen on hard times and could no longer raise financial support, so he returned to Nasik to live. On 16 February 1944, D.G. Phalke died penniless and forgotten. A few years earlier, when the magazine *Moving Picture Monthly* informed him of a special issue they intended to publish on him, Phalke replied, 'The industry to which I gave birth has forgotten me, why do you try to remember me? It is in the nature of the world to forget. You may also do the same.'

P.K. Nair, one of India's leading film historians, believes that D.G. Phalke chose mythology for the cinema not only because it was an easy means of communicating to the largest number of people, but also because Phalke saw mythological stories as a way of evoking patriotic feelings in the Indian nation at a time when the country was a British colony. By showing Lord Krishna overcoming the demon snake Kamsa in his 1919 film *Kaliya Mardan*, Phalke showed that it was possible to fight the powerful and to challenge the imperialism that had plundered the nation in the same way the demon snake had poisoned the sacred river.

Around 1,300 films were made during the silent era. Only thirteen of these have survived, of which about half are incomplete, and these are preserved at the National Film Archives in Pune. P.K. Nair himself has been instrumental in saving some rare classics. In 1970, he travelled to Nasik, and with the help of a friend and Phalke's sons, recovered sixteen cans of nitrate film containing Phalke's seventh film, *Kaliya Mardan*, from the top of an old cupboard. On entering D.G. Phalke's home, P.K. Nair noticed that over the doorway, where traditionally a figure of a God is placed to welcome visitors, Phalke had nailed a wooden replica of a camera. P.K. Nair has worked hard to encourage the perception in India that films are an art form that merit preservation and not only a commercial commodity to be exploited for immediate cash. It took years for Indian producers to understand the value of cinema and it was only through government initiatives that the National Film Archives of India was created in 1964. P.K. Nair was its first director and maintains that Indian cinema could not have started with any subject other than the mythological:

P.K. Nair: Long before cinema came to India, most of the entertainment forms – whether folk forms, dance or musical recitals – have had a strong association with the temple or with some form of religious activity. In fact, one of the reasons people would go to the temple, apart from the fact they wanted to pray, was that they could watch a long *Kathakali* performance or a *Nautanki* [a play] once the worship was over. These performances had their origins in mythology and were adaptations of episodes from the Hindu epics, the *Mahabharat* and the

Ramayan. So entertainment and the performing arts always had strong roots in religion and religious values. When you go to the temple with the entire family, you wear your best dress, and there's a tremendous joyous feeling. In the same way, you'd go with the whole family to watch a film. In the early days of cinema, the audience would sit on the sand spread on the floor of the tent where the film was projected. And the audience would see a film based on religion or was inspired by religion. If you stay awake all night watching this kind of performance, a part of you is involved with the values associated with religious thought – it's a kind of a pilgrimage. So you are participating in a form of spiritual experience. The mythological films were not entertainment in the escapist sense, they were part of the experience of growing up. However crudely the film was made, the fact was that we were watching something that was largely acceptable by society. If you look at Indian cinema until the talkies, more than sixty or seventy per cent of the films had something to do with mythology. I remember my father used to tell me to see a film like *Raja Harishchandra*, because for him, it was as good as reading a book or going to school.

In the silent era, eighty per cent of the films produced were made in the Bombay Presidency (as it was known then), followed by Bengal and the South. The 1920s saw the early work of several important Indian filmmakers and studio owners including D.N. Sampat (Kohinoor Film Company), Chandulal Shah (Ranjit Movietone), J.F. Madan (Elphinstone Bioscope Company,

Calcutta) and the gifted Baburao Painter (Maharasthra Film Company, Kohlapur), whose apprentices included the celebrated filmmakers V. Shantaram, V. Damle and S. Fatehlal. Himanshu Rai and Franz Osten (a German who lived in India until the war years, when he was obliged to leave) were also key filmmakers of the time, producing individually styled and authored films. Osten's *Light of Asia* (1925, *Prem Sanyas*) was based on the Edwin Arnold poem on the life of Gautama Buddha, his *Shiraz* (1928) tells the story of how the Emperor Shahjahan came to build the Taj Mahal, while his *Throw of Dice* (1929, *Prapancha Pash*) was inspired by an episode in the *Mahabharat* concerning the perils of gambling.

Aside from the mythological, the 1920s saw the birth of other film genres, such as the social film (examples include *Our Hindustan* [1928] and *Orphan Daughter*), the historical film celebrating Rajput history and grandeur, the stunt film based on the Hollywood model, and Muslim subjects inspired by Persian love legends including *Laila Majnu* and stories set in the splendour of Moghul courts. The Persian love stories depended on family conflict, court intrigue, poetic dialogue, and songs of love and lament and these were better served by cinema after the birth of sound. The films with Muslim subjects were later developed into the 'Muslim Social', of which the author Shahrukh Husain commented, 'Predictably, Muslim Socials were about Indian Muslims and were the forum for the portrayal of many social institutions of the exotic upper and lower classes of this community.' (*The Cambridge Encyclopedia of India*, 1989, Cambridge University Press).

Another popular genre starting in the silent era was the action film. The lack of sound in cinema did not hamper the exploits of action heroes, who needed no dialogue to show their mettle, and there were a number of these, including the muscle-man Gangaram, the swashbuckling hero Jairaj, who started his career with *Sparkling Youth* (1930, *Jagmati Jawani*) and who was a gymnast and sportsman, and Eddie Billimoria, who fought villains and vagabonds in films such as *Rogue Of Rajasthan* (1930) and *Naughty But Nice*. Eddie Billimoria, in the role of a cowboy, also introduced a short-lived trend of westerns made in India. Other directors who made stunt movies included Nanubhai Desai of Paramount Studios and Kikubhai Desai. It is no surprise that Kikubhai Desai's son, Manmohan Desai, would make the kind of action films he did in the 1970s, bearing in mind his father's style of movie-making. The filmmakers who were largely responsible for popularizing the stunt film were J.B.H. Wadia and his brother Homi Wadia, of Wadia Movietone. They became the kings of this genre, starting with the railroad thriller *Toofan Mail* (1932), which featured several fight sequences staged on the roof of a moving train. The Wadias loved Hollywood and were directly inspired by American serials, westerns and slapstick comedies. Their most famous star was the queen of the forties action movie, Fearless Nadia.

The stunt film and the adventure action film did not appeal to everyone: the educated classes saw them as populist, vulgar and a corrupting influence. This division in film styles is why distributors and producers continue to see Hindi films as being of two main categories: 'films for the classes and films for the masses'. The assumption was that the upper classes, who were more educated, expected something substantial from cinema, whereas the poor looked to cinema as pure entertainment.

Amitabh Bachchan: I was born in 1942 and cinema in those days was something that was looked down upon. It was considered taboo in the so-called higher strata of society and by the more refined, educated elite. I don't know which category I belonged to, but I was made to believe that cinema was not good and therefore should be avoided. This seemed to be the general feeling in the entire country. Women from good homes, for example, were not allowed to go to the movies, and if they wanted to work in films, they were treated as outcasts. Acting for women was regarded a profession for women of dubious repute. The films we got to see were vetted and screened by our parents – if they had an educational or historical value, or were mythologicals based on the *Ramayan* or the *Mahabharat,* or based on any other religious stories, that was all right. But other than that, for sheer entertainment, cinema wasn't a good thing.

Another important role fulfilled by the mythological was that it gave Indian audiences instant access to cinema. The fact that people were brought up on these multi-layered stories meant that audiences did not need dialogues to follow complicated narratives. Grandmothers told grandchildren about the legends of Krishna defeating Kamsa, Harishchandra being returned his kingdom and Hanuman's brave fight to destroy Lanka. Another essential element in this connection between film and ancient myth was that by adapting the mythological to the screen, Indian filmmakers could play between the new and the familiar, using the Western invention of cinema to tell Indian stories. This balancing out of the predictable and the innovative is the pillar of popular cinema everywhere in the world, equally determining the strength of Hollywood and Hong Kong productions. Reverting to the tried and tested holds true even in 2001, as Javed Akhtar confirms when he observes that most producers still ask him to 'write a completely original script that has come before'.

Mythological stories offered filmmakers fabulous visual opportunities – what could be more magical than bringing to life a God performing some great miracle? An excellent example is Phalke's *Kaliya Mardan*, featuring a terrific underwater fight sequence between Krishna and Kamsa, the demon snake. Phalke was as talented as Georges Meliès in bringing about magical scenes in movies. A later example is the wonderful 1938 film *Gopal Krishna* directed by the ingenious V. Damle and S. Fatehlal. The film tells the story of young Lord Krishna saving a village from demons that try to destroy it by sending down a storm and floods. Krishna covers the flooded village with the Mount Govardhan and all the village folk run under the mountain for cover. The special effects in the film are extraordinary for their time, while the film's photography, the editing, and its use of background music to highlight action are first rate, and show how gifted and innovative the early Indian filmmakers were despite the limited technical means at their disposal.

Devotional films formed another extremely popular cine-matic genre, which came into its own in the 1930s. They were based on the lives of Hindu poet-saints who were linked to the Bhakti tradition. Originating in the seventh and eighth centuries, Bhakti is based on the direct connection between a devotee and his or her God, in contrast to the orchestrated rigour of Brahmanic rituals. In the fifteenth and sixteenth centuries, the teachings of poet-saints such as the Muslim-born weaver Kabir made a deep impact, winning the hearts of the peasantry and artisans, as did the songs of Mirabai, the sixteenth-century Krishna devotee. The Bhakti tradition had a literary and religious form in both north and south India and was revived once again in the nineteenth century by nationalists and egalitarian reformists. The classic film *Sant Tukaram* (1936, V. Damle and S. Fatehlal) is the best example of the devotional film. It is based on the life on Tukaram, a celebrated Marathi poet-saint. Although the devotional film has virtually disappeared, many Hindi films include scenes involving prayer or the singing of devotional songs from both the Bhakti (the *bhajan*) and the Sufi (the *qawwali*) traditions.

The Hindu epics may have offered a wealth of stories for filmmakers to choose from, but certain tales about popular deities and divine characters found public favour more readily than others and these were used again and again. Particularly popular were stories about the Gods Krishna, Ganesh and Hanuman, the actions of Goddess Lakshmi and the self-sacrificing dedication of women, as exemplified in S.N. Patankar's *Sati Anjani* (1922) and *Sati Vijaya* (1931). ('Sati' is a Hindi word referring to the practice whereby a woman sacrifices herself by dying on her husband's funeral pyre, and it also signifies a chaste and virtuous woman.) The story of the most dutiful woman of all was *Sati Savitri*, which has been filmed several times since 1931.

The virtues and strengths of righteous and religious characters became part of the cinema experience and contributed towards the definition of human heroism. Director Dharmesh Darshan believes the film hero is still a reworking of the mythological hero:

Dharmesh Darshan: There are certain virtues that define an Indian hero and these have come from the great epics. A hero should be the 'Adarsh Purush' – that is what the great Lord Ram used to be called. 'Adarsh Purush' means 'the perfect male'. First of all, he should be the perfect son, because the family and the parent structure is very important in India. He should be the ideal husband, the ideal lover, the ideal warrior. And when he achieves these ideals, he has to be extremely moral, but not judgmental. The hero's morality is a personal issue; if he tries to carry it like a cross and make others suffer for it, he's no longer a hero. In that way, the Indian hero is very progressive. His personal character is very strong and he's always helping others. He's not judging people by their circumstances, by their birth. He judges the villain by his actions, that tell the hero 'here's a negative guy'. So he's quite fascinating, this Indian hero. He's really the best of what a man should be. Indians are basically dreamers and the hero is what every man wants to be, and every woman wants to fantasize about.

The mythological film was not only used as a reference for screen heroes and heroines, but also helped cinema to overcome the many social, caste and linguistic barriers that exist in India. Phalke dealt with the linguistic problem by using title cards that in some cases featured two languages (English and Hindi), and when he made films of particular interest to Maharastrians, he used cards in Marathi. The idea of bilingual title cards was taken up by other filmmakers during the silent period, and up to four languages were used, if required.

Indian silent films weren't really silent – as in Hollywood, live musicians provided a soundtrack. The English language films shown in India's big cities had a violinist and pianist providing the music. This two-member orchestra was usually musicians from Goa – a Portuguese colony at that time – who had studied music and could sight-read. The harmonium and the tabla were the main instruments played with Indian silent films. In his article 'Sound in a Silent Era', celebrated music scholar Bhaskar Chandavarkar notes that 'The harmonium and tabla players were not only the first music directors, but also dialogue writers and dubbers, as they were expected to stamp their feet, shout and trigger excitement during the action scenes, crying "*Maro*" ["Hit him"], "*Chup, saale*" ["Shut up, you bastard"] or "*Khamosh*" ["Silence!"] while the villain got what was coming to him' (*Cinema Vision*, Vol. 1, January 1980).

Though this genre continued to have a healthy life in south India, in Hindi cinema the mythological had virtually disappeared by the 1950s. Later, at the height of 1970s action and vendetta films, Vijay Sharma's low-budget movie *Jai Santoshi Maa* broke all box-office records by becoming one of the biggest hits of 1975 (along with blockbusters such as *Sholay* and *Deewaar*). This film made Santoshi Maa, a little-known Goddess, into a hugely popular icon and many people throughout India kept a fast, or *vrat*, in her name. The film's popularity was so extraordinary that it later became the subject of academic study by Indian and international scholars: the anthropologist Veena Das analysed the film in her essay 'The Mythological Film and its Framework of Meaning' (1980), while American scholar Stanley Kurtz examined its influence and impact in 'All the Mothers Are One' (published by Columbia University Press in 1992). *Jai Santoshi Maa*'s heroine, Satyavati, is a Cinderella-like character, devoted to the Goddess but persecuted by two terrible sisters-in-law. Satyavati's life is a hard one, but every time she is further victimised, Santoshi Maa comes to her aid. The young disciple fasts in the name of Santoshi Maa, imploring her in song, 'Accept my humble fast, O Mother. Why must your child weep so in this cruel world. Change the course of my destiny, Mother Santoshi.'

Anita Guha, who played the role of Santoshi Maa, remembers the extraordinary impact that the film had on Indian cinema-goers: 'Audiences were showering coins, flower petals and rice at the screen in appreciation of the film. They entered the cinema barefoot and set up a small temple outside the cinema. In Bandra, where mythological films aren't shown, it ran for fifty weeks. It was a miracle.' Anita Guha was mobbed every time she went out, and her appearance was frequently accompanied by the cry, 'Maa, there goes Maa'. Moreover, even when the film's run ended, audiences refused to allow their local cinemas to take down the huge cut-outs showing the Goddess.

P.K. Nair: Associating the screen image with the real actor isn't new. It started in the late 1930s and the early 1940s, when we had this very popular image of Rama and Sita – Sita was played by Shobhana Samarth and Ram was played by Prem Adeeb. Now mind you, Prem Adeeb was not a Hindu but people didn't know that, in fact it was kept a secret. So they acted in Vijay Bhatt's wonderful trilogy starting with *Bharat Milap* [1942], *Ram Rajya* [1945], and *Rambaan* [1948]. It's said that these are the only films Gandhiji saw and liked. I remember seeing calendars with pictures of Ram and Sita in the image of Prem Adeeb and Shobhana Samarth. People would garland the calendar image and pray to it. What is important in the Indian context is representation. Nobody is concerned with the real. So your association is with an image, and this image represents a God and the values attributed to that God. That is why we also worship stones – like the Shiv Lingam. It has no resemblance to the actual figure of Shiva. But this image or figure allows you to focus spiritual thoughts and after that, the image does not matter at all – it's only a starting point.

Although audiences lost their fascination with the mythological film in the 1950s, its influence on stories and characters can be seen in dozens of key Hindi films. In Raj Kapoor's *Awaara*, Judge Raghunath (Prithviraj Kapoor) suspects that his wife, Leela (Leela Chitnis), is no longer 'pure' because she has been kidnapped by Jagga (K.N. Singh), a bandit once charged with rape. Leela returns home after a few months and is pregnant. This is a direct reference to the *Ramayan*, in which Sita is kidnapped by the demon Ravan and will only be accepted back into society when she goes through the test of fire to prove to the *Praja* (the public) that she is still pure. Raj Kapoor makes this reference explicit through a fabulously atmospheric song that tells us of Leela's desperate plight as she is thrown out of her home by her suspecting husband: 'You sent away the virtuous Sita, you sent her into exile, why did the earth and the sky not open and cry in protest?'

P.K. Nair believes that it isn't only mythological characters themselves that have influenced Hindi film heroes in subsequent years, but also the relationships they have with each other. Conflicts between families that cause a rift to separate them, harks back to the fight between the Pandavas and the Kauravas in the *Mahabharat*; the theme of brothers who are in conflict echoes Karna and Arjuna's relationship. The mythological themes are reworked in modern settings and reappear in nearly every decade of film production. Actress Bela Bose, who starred as one of the cruel sisters in *Jai Santoshi Maa*, believes the mythological is 'a river that will never run dry' and so will return to the big screen. In the 1980s, the mythological became a phenomenon of the small screen when television series based on the *Ramayan* and the *Mahabharat* captured the imaginations of millions of people all over again.

Javed Akhtar: The mythological films were true to the traditional narrative and they didn't experiment with that at all. This traditional narrative has been re-worked over the centuries and is so perfect and so foolproof that I don't think there is much scope for further improvising. The narratives of the *Ramayan* or the *Mahabharat* are really mind-blowing. These epic tales have been made increasingly dramatic over the years, so how can any scriptwriter improve on them? As a matter of fact, they are a reference point for Indian writers. They are great scripts in themselves. Mythologicals were also produced for television, starting with Ramanand Sagar's series of the *Ramayan,* and then the *Mahabharat* made by B.R. Chopra. These series had ratings that a Western media person might not believe. The *Mahabharat* had ninety-eight per cent viewing figures. That's unheard of. Streets used to be deserted all over India when the *Ramayan* or the *Mahabharat* was on air.

The mythological film was the perfect means for cinema to become accepted during the silent era. But what kind of Indian film could maintain this strong link with audiences when sound came to the Indian screen in 1931? Over 150 million people at that time understood Hindustani (a mix of Hindi and Urdu, also known as the language of the bazaar) and as the first talkie was to be made in Bombay, Hindustani was chosen over the fourteen official Indian languages to be the lingua franca of popular cinema. Once the language question had been resolved, films looked to the Urdu Parsee Theatre for subject matter. Ardeshir Irani, who made India's first sound film (*Alam Ara* [1931]), admitted that the idea of making an Indian talkie came from Universal Pictures' production of *Show Boat*, which was a forty per cent talkie. Interviewed in 1949 by film historian B.D. Garga, Ardeshir Irani explains the problems they faced filming with sound: 'In those days we completed a silent film in a month or so. But *Alam Ara* took months because of the hazards of sound recording under very trying conditions. Besides, we had to be very careful not to disclose the fact that we were making a talkie. It was a closely guarded secret.' Based on Joseph David's Urdu Parsee play, *Alam Ara* is a costume drama telling the story of the rivalry of two queens and involving many characters, plots and subplots. The film was released on 14 March 1931 at the Majestic Cinema and its songs immediately proved a smash, particularly the one sung by actor/singer W.M. Khan in the role of a fakir, '*De de Khuda ke naam par pyare*' ('Give alms in the name of Allah'). Thereafter, songs and dances were established as an integral part of Indian popular cinema.

Alam Ara fully embraced the conventions of the Urdu Parsee Theatre. Girish Karnad, celebrated actor and playwright both for screen and stage, explains how the Parsee Theatre itself came to be:

Girish Karnad: Most people overlook the fact that the great transition in Indian performing arts is linked to the creation by the British of three cities: Bombay, Calcutta, Madras. What distinguishes Bombay or Calcutta from Delhi, Mysore, Nagpur or Hyderabad is that in public life you have to pretend to be an Englishman [*laughs*]. In private life you may not be. You had to believe in merit-ocracy, you didn't accept caste, you had to believe that individualism was the right thing, and caste and family loyalties were supposed to be secondary. So these cities bring an entirely new thinking to culture itself, and you had to accept the British definition of culture. This completely transformed the attitude to performing arts, particularly to the theatre.

The playwright in India had never been looked upon as representative of culture. Poets, yes; philosophers, yes. For example, Kalidas is admired as a great play-wright but he would not have been considered repre-sentative of Indian culture until the nineteenth century. So in the nineteenth century you suddenly see Kalidas being seen as the Indian Shakespeare and translations of his works are staged, including *Shakuntala*. This is the whole colonial experience – on one side you admire them and you also hate them. The interesting thing about Shakespeare is Indians loved Shakespeare. They learned from him.

Until the nineteenth century, performers were looked down upon – men too, they always came from the lower castes. In the nineteenth century, it begins to change. You get Nawab Wajid Ali Shah doing *Indarsabha*, a play in which he himself dances with dancing girls. He was influenced by the French form called 'tableau'. The British also encouraged their women to act – that was a great revolution to Indians. It showed that acting was a respectable thing, although Indians were not allowed to enter clubs to see these performances. During the British times, Victorian theatre companies used to come to India and they would stage plays. Not Shakespeare, but melodramas by the French playwright, Scribe. He wrote thundering curtain lines and last-minute-rescue dramas.

There was another English playwright called Sardou, whom Shaw dismissed as 'Sardoudeedum'. Victorian theatre introduced the proscenium to India – curtains rolling up to reveal a stage – and within the proscenium, a lot of stage machinery, stage effects. My father would tell me in many scenes, a cannon would blast, boom! And the scene would change. They had women shooting out of cannons. The idea of spectacle. This was the Victorian theatre, and the Parsee Theatre learnt the construction of dramatic tension in plays from playwrights like Scribe and Sardou. First the romance, the couple fall in love, then problems arise, then misunderstanding and then the tense build-up. Very often the couple is saved at the last minute with the thundering curtain line. This is in a way Shakespeare gone haywire and that was the main fare of the Victorians.

This form was picked up by the Parsee Theatre, to which they added music and song coming from the Bhakti and Sufi tradition. The Parsee Theatre itself is an example of secularism, the British kind of secularism. The owners who financed the plays performed in Gujarati were Parsees. Then they discovered that the reach would be greater if the plays were written in Urdu, so they had Muslim writers such as Agha Hashar Kashmiri. But most of the audience was Hindu, so they also produced mythologicals. This is typical of the concoction in Hindi film production.

These narrative forms, including the Urdu Parsee plays, Hindu mythologicals, music, song and dance, action and stunt, the social film, the Muslim historical and the romantic film, which were treated as separate genres in early movies, were regularly being mixed together by the 1940s into a single picture, establishing for ever the prototype of the Hindi film. And while many film directors merely turned out formulaic films containing these elements, the more talented ones understood how to use these conventions in traditional ways yet produce notably individual films.

Chapter Six

CALLING THE SHOTS

Every period of Indian cinema has had its share of excellent directors. The names of V. Shantaram, P.C. Barua, Sohrab Modi, J.B.H. Wadia, Nitin Bose, Debaki Bose and Kidar Sharma, to name but a few, are associated with some of the finest Hindi movies. No one will forget the majestic and splendid *Mughal-e-Azam*, directed by K. Asif in 1960, who made the film his life's work, and the films of Kamaal Amrohi (*Pakeezah* and *Mahal*) will long be remembered for their originality and exquisitely refined atmosphere. The same can be said of Manmohan Desai's marvellous *Amar Akbar Anthony* and Ramesh Sippy's tour de force *Sholay*. The fine work of other directors, such as Nasir Hussain, Subodh Mukherji, Shakti Samanta, Vijay Anand, Raj Khosla and Hrishikesh Mukherjee, has not been duly recognized. But ask any Hindi cinema fan, or film practitioner for that matter, to choose a favourite director and they will most likely choose one of the greats from the 1950s: Mehboob Khan, Bimal Roy, Raj Kapoor or Guru Dutt. Retrospectives of their work have travelled the world, astounding audiences everywhere who expect Hindi cinema to be loud and vulgar. The cinematic impact these filmmakers have had is profound, influencing every generation of filmmaker since their time. Karan Johar, who is considered one of the most successful and talented young directors today (and he's still under thirty), is among those moved by their work.

Karan Johar: What attracted me to cinema was the magic of Raj Kapoor, the brilliance of Guru Dutt, the magnitude of Mehboob Khan, and the reality of Bimal Roy. Their work made me want to make films, and also the works of another great director, Satyajit Ray. I used to watch their films and think, 'Oh God, can I ever do something that's even close to this?' I have seen all those great Indian films and I feel there is a real lack of films of that calibre today. I feel we young filmmakers must bring another golden period to Indian cinema – something that hasn't happened since the fifties. We can't call any other period – for example, the seventies or the eighties – a golden period. Subsequently, it's been a complete downfall for Indian cinema – we have one or two films that stand out every year, but that's it.

Mehboob Khan was born into a modest family in Bilimora, Gujarat, as Ramzan Khan on 7 September 1906. Mehboob had no formal education, but from an early age he developed an overriding passion for movies. At the age of sixteen he ran away to Bombay, hoping to find work as an actor. However, he did not manage to get beyond the gates of the city's leading studio, the Imperial Film Company, and was promptly brought back home by his father. Khan senior married his son to young Fatima, who was of a similar humble and modest background to the Khans. Undeterred, after the birth of his first son, Ayub, in 1927, Mehboob ran away again, his keenness to enter the film world as strong as ever. A family friend introduced him to Ardeshir Irani, founder of the Imperial Film Company and director of India's first talkie, 1931's *Alam Ara*. Irani was impressed by Mehboob and gave him a part as one of the forty thieves in *Ali Baba aur Chalis Chor* (1932). At this early stage in his career, Mehboob dreamed of becoming a lead actor, although this was never to happen. He worked as an assistant to R.S. Chaudhury before Ardeshir Irani let him direct *Al Hilal* (1934/35, *Judgement of Allah*), through Irani's new company, Sagar Movietone – the film was a huge success and Mehboob's life as a director was up and running.

Early on in his career, Mehboob Khan found the ideal team, with whom he worked throughout his life, including cameraman Fareedoon Irani, writers Wajahat Mirza, Agha Jani Kashmiri and later Zia Sarhadi, Ali Raza, music director Naushad Ali and lyricists Majrooh Sultanpuri and Shakeel Badayuni. Contemporary director Dharmesh Darshan observes that the great directors of yesteryear were men of vision who skilfully used talented teams of specialists to make their visions become a reality:

Dharmesh Darshan: In the old days, the filmmaker was the author. These days many directors depend on different people for different sections of the film. So they will have a dance director, a fight master and so on. That's not how I work, I have a great team, I have a dance director and an action director, but we work together.

We have long screenplays, we use many locations, we have songs, our films are three and a half hours long. Sometimes a film takes three years to complete. Nowadays, things are improving – we try to finish a film in a year or two. It's basically an undisciplined industry. Here the filmmaker has to do everything, he has to handle people all the way and get his various members of the unit together to achieve his vision. I believe the director is the captain of the ship, he should be responsible for the film's failure or success. And this was the way all the great filmmakers worked.

Mehboob Khan later made several important films at the National Studios, including *Aurat* and *Roti* (1942, *Bread*). *Aurat*, inspired both by Pearl S. Buck's novel *The Good Earth* and by Maxim Gorky's *Mother*, is a story about an exemplary village woman called Radha (played by Sardar Akhtar – later to become Mehboob's second wife), who survives against the odds in order to raise her two sons. In 1957, Mehboob Khan remade this film as *Mother India*. The highly unusual and innovative *Roti* was told in part by a narrator, the cynical Ashraf Khan, whose songs were a scathing comment on contemporary life, designed to encourage revolt.

In 1943, Mehboob Khan launched his own company, Mehboob Productions. The production company's intriguing emblem of a hammer and sickle is accompanied by a voice-over stating, '*Muddai laakh bura chaahe to kyaa hotaa hai, vahi hotaa hai jo manzur-e-Khuda hotaa hai*' ('No matter if the plaintiff wishes you a hundred ills, it is Allah's will alone that determines what befalls you'). The interesting juxtaposition of contradictory ideologies, social and religious, seems to represent Mehboob's head and heart respectively. The same contrast is found in his film oeuvre, which ranges from the socialistic *Roti* to the romantic *Najma* (1943) with its cultured finesse and genteel etiquette. In a 1957 article in *Filmfare*, Mehboob Khan comments on his choice of insignia: 'I took the hammer and sickle as our symbol because we considered ourselves workers and not just producers, directors and stars. I have been accused of being a communist for using this symbol, but those who know me well know that I am no communist.'

Mehboob's *Andaaz* is a most extraordinary film, and one of the first Hindi films to ever deal with the psychology of emotions. One major underlying theme of the work juxtaposes the behavioural nuances of the westernized, liberal middle class against the traditional Indian expectations of how men and women are supposed to relate to one another. Released in 1949, within two years of India's independence and Partition, *Andaaz* had a look quite unlike any other Indian film. Its opulent setting, sophisticated plot and character development is on a par with the best American melodramas made by Ernst Lubitsch, King Vidor or Douglas Sirk. Mehboob Khan builds both major and small scenes with great sensitivity, bringing layers of meaning to this love triangle involving Nina (Nargis), the rejected lover Dilip (Dilip Kumar) and Nina's husband, Rajan (Raj Kapoor). Mehboob is subtle in his treatment of melodrama, underplaying the heightened emotions that dominate so many Hindi films. Instead of the usual outcries of the broken-hearted lover, Dilip's anguish is expressed through soft and ghostly singing that floats through the room as Nina stands by the window on her wedding night. The subconscious voice expressed in the form of the song runs through her heart: '*Kya paaya hai loot ke tu ne, ek gareeb ka pyar*' ('What did you gain by robbing a humble man of his love?'), creating one of Hindi cinema's most stirring moments.

In 1952, Mehboob made *Aan,* a romantic costume drama filmed in colour. Colour processing wasn't available in India in those days, so he shot the movie on 16mm Kodachrome colour stock and had it blown up to 35mm at Technicolor's London laboratory. Peter Pitt, an assistant editor, who worked with Mehboob Khan in London early in 1952 on the final soundtrack of the film, recalled working on *Aan* in a 1989 article in *The Film & Television Technician*:

> **Peter Pitt**: Mehboob would not screen more than a couple of reels at a time in a preview theatre as he was very concerned about who might see it. Why he should have been so worried, nobody knew, it was long before the days of video pirating. Mehboob Khan was a devout Muslim, and at certain times during the day, he would lay out a small mat on the cutting room floor and kneel and pray. This was all done without a word to the British crew who, at first, were not sure what they should do, such as whether to continue working; but as this became a regular occurrence, they just lowered the volume of sound from the moviolas and carried on with the job.

The land in Bandra, a rich suburb of Bombay, which was used as the location for *Aan*'s royal arena, finally became Mehboob Studios and is one of the last Bombay studios left today. It is now run by Mehboob's two sons, Iqbal and Shaukat, and many blockbuster films have been shot there. Following the success of *Aan*, Mehboob directed one of his rare box-office failures, 1954's *Amar*, a film that he considered his personal favourite. At the age of fifty, Mehboob made his nineteenth film, *Mother India*, a remake of his original *Aurat*. This time, he cast Nargis in the lead role of Radha. He elaborated on the theme of this extraordinary film in *Filmfare* in 1957: 'I have always had the most profound respect for Indian womanhood. The story of *Aurat,* as visualized by me and developed by Babubhai Mehta, was centred around the fact that the true Indian woman enters her husband's home when she marries and leaves it only when she dies, that she will never sell her chastity for any price on earth. I thought of remaking *Aurat* in the context of the changing world. But the main character has not changed – the Indian woman who is one with the land she works on.' *Mother India* is perhaps the most influential Indian film of all time, providing archetypal characters and a template for dramatic conflict that has been reworked by dozens of directors and writers since.

The great director once described what cinema meant to him: 'Work is a religion with me, and films are my first love. No one who interferes with my work is ever spared my temper and displeasure.' Mehboob Khan's enthusiasm for filmmaking stayed with him throughout his life; one of his long-cherished ambitions was to make a film based on the story of the Taj Mahal. Sadly, the project was destined to remain a dream – on 28 May 1964 he suffered a heart attack and died at the age of fifty-eight. He passed away the day after Prime Minister Pandit Jawaharlal Nehru, a man whom Mehboob admired all his life. In his private office at Mehboob Studios a picture still hangs showing the smiling Nehru with Mehboob Khan.

The other director who started his career in the studio era of
the 1930s was Bimal Roy. Born in Dhaka, East Bengal, in 1909
(now Bangladesh), he belonged to an aristocratic landowning
family, but when the family fortunes began to dwindle the young
Roy moved to Calcutta to find work. He was taken on at the New
Theatres as an apprentice and soon became assistant cameraman. In 1935, when P.C. Barua made *Devdas*, he asked Bimal
Roy to photograph it, and the relationship proved so successful
that Roy went on to film most of Barua's famous works. A few
years later, B.N. Sircar, the owner of the New Theatres, gave
Roy his first film, *Udayer Pathey* (1944, 'The Path to Sunrise') to
direct. *Udayer Pathey* is a film about the exploitation of the
lower-middle classes by the rich and was a big success, making
Bimal Roy a celebrity overnight. Mrs Manobina Roy, his wife,
remembers those early years in Calcutta and Bombay:

Manobina Roy: The New Theatres was an old institution
run by B.N. Sircar. It was like a kingdom, everyone who
belonged to the studio gave their allegiance and loyalty
to Sircar. But they ran into money trouble. People were
moving to Bombay by 1951 and we moved as well. A
friend of my husband's, Hiten Choudhury, who was also
from Dhaka, introduced us to Devika Rani of Bombay
Talkies. When she left Bombay Talkies, Ashok Kumar
and others took over and they invited my husband to
make *Maa* with Bharat Bhushan.

Then in 1953 he made *Parineeta*, which was based
on a novel by Sarat Chandra Chatterji. It was a beautiful,
romantic and gentle story. My husband insisted that his
team join him from Calcutta, and so Hrishikesh

Mukherjee, who was an editor then, the comedian Asit Sen, Pal Mahendra, Nabendu Ghosh, Nasir Hussain and later the music director, Salil Choudhury and the cameraman Kamal Bose, who shot all my husband's films, joined us. We were all together in a house in Malad where Devika Rani once lived, a five-minute walk away from the Bombay Talkies studios.

My husband's family were *zamindars* [landlords] and they had lost everything, but he did not care about property. He used to say that *zamindars* were big tyrants and he wanted nothing to do with them. You can see the same attitude running through *Udayer Pathey* and *Do Bigha Zameen*. In 1953, *Filmfare* started giving awards called the Clare Awards, named after Ms Clare of *The Times of India* [later, they became known as the *Filmfare* awards]. Ms Clare had this brilliant idea of instituting annual awards on the lines of the Oscars. And *Filmfare* had given Bimal Roy the Best Director and Best Picture awards for *Do Bigha Zameen*. It was a very moving day for us. When my husband went up on stage, I heard whispering around me: 'Who is this Bengali lad, standing there in his *dhoti kurta*? He makes a film on the slums and gets an award.' After the ceremony, Raj Kapoor, who had lived in Calcutta where his father worked in the New Theatres, was the first to come up to my husband and hug him, saying, 'Bimalda ['Da' is a term of respect in Bengali, meaning elder brother], you've done it!' Click, click, click, all the cameras snapped.

Bimal Roy made some extraordinary and compassionate films; he told his stories through dialogue, but depended equally on visual imagery to provide a clear and simple narrative thread. In *Sujata*, a close-up of Nutan's face tells us as much about her plight as any dialogue explaining her low-caste birth would. The most unusual aspect of Bimal Roy's work was his use of sound, and he was one of the few Bombay filmmakers to really use it to create atmosphere. In *Madhumati*, the hero Anand (Dilip Kumar) listens out for the cry of the tiniest bird as he walks on the winding roads of a remote hill station – all of nature speaks to him before he sings the beautiful '*Suhaanaa safar aur yeh mausam haseen*' ('The journey is wondrous and the season divine'). Roy knew how to use song effectively in the narrative. He created many of his musical moments by holding wide shots and close-ups for a long time, allowing the tune and the lyrics, more than camera movements and fast cutting, to determine the pace and rhythm. Bimal Roy's films are replete with fine moments of cinematic mood and his direction of actors is marvellous – the great Dilip Kumar's best work is found in the films he did for Mehboob Khan and Bimal Roy. Indeed, Dilip Kumar's performance in Roy's *Devdas* became a benchmark for later actors.

> **Dilip Kumar:** Devdas was all bound in tradition, he does not have the courage to rebel. He loves Parvati tremendously, he punishes her and he punishes himself. He couldn't assert himself and do what would be regarded as quite simple by prevailing standards. His crisis was made more acute because that was a time when no man or woman could think of doing anything against the authority of elders.

Bimal Roy had great sensitivity – it wasn't in the spoken word, but in the quiet interludes. He disliked speech and he would cut as much verbiage as possible. For example, take the scene when Devdas returns from Calcutta as a grown man and goes to see Paro. The night is falling, she hears his footsteps and shyly retreats into the courtyard and runs up the stairs to her room. Now, this is the director's ingenuity: he has Paro light a *diya* [lamp] and as she lights this *diya*, the light falls on her face, and the camera slowly tilts up to reveal the face of Devdas, who has followed her to her room. Light falls on their faces, they see each other for the first time as grown adults, and there is silence. In the film, Devdas speaks little and Parvati even less. As an actor, the question in *Devdas* was of trying not to do, rather than doing.

Another of Bimal Roy's achievements was to introduce new subjects to cinema. He was one of the few Bombay-based directors (probably because of his own Bengali background) to have adapted literary works to the screen. He turned two other Sarat Chandra Chatterji novels into films besides *Devdas* – *Parineeta* and *Biraj Bahu* (1954). *Kabuliwala* and *Do Bigha Zameen* were shot in Calcutta, and his *Sujata* and *Bandini*, with the excellent Nutan, also had Bengali subjects. Bimal Roy created his own production company, and the film that made him the most money was *Madhumati* (1958), a ghost story written by Ritwik Ghatak starring Dilip Kumar as the hero, Anand, and Vyjayantimala as Madhumati and her two reincarnations. The film is beautifully mysterious and made doubly atmospheric by

Bimal Roy's clever use of sound. In the concluding scene, Anand follows Madhumati's call (she appears now in ghost form) through an old haunted mansion with huge staircases and series of arched corridors (reminiscent of sets in German expressionist films). Anand finally ends up on an open terrace where, in the dark night, the rain is pouring down. Madhumati is standing on the parapet and beckons Anand to join her in death.

The most famous of all Bimal Roy's films is the heartfelt and poignant *Do Bigha Zameen* ('Two Acres of Land') with Balraj Sahni, Nirupa Roy, Rattan Kumar and Meena Kumari (in a minor role). The film is the story of a poor farmer, Shambhu Mahato (brilliantly played by Balraj Sahni), who must go to Calcutta to earn money to pay back a cheating landlord (Murad) in order to save his land. Shambhu and his son (Rattan Kumar) land up in Calcutta, where they live in a slum, with Shambhu working as a rickshaw puller. The film's most famous scene shows a dehumanized Shambhu with a client in his hand-rickshaw urging him to catch up with his girlfriend who is in the rickshaw ahead. Shambhu has to run as fast as a galloping horse in order to earn a few rupees. Despite all his efforts, at the end of the film, Shambhu Mahato loses his land. *Do Bigha Zameen* remains one of the defining films of Hindi cinema.

Bimal Roy was a pious man, and during the last years of his life he became increasingly spiritual. He died on 8 January 1966 of lung cancer, at the age of fifty-seven. He won eleven *Filmfare* awards, the highest number given to any Hindi cinema director. Years after his death, his colleagues, family and friends remember him as a soft-spoken yet persuasive man who was always moved by the plight of the downtrodden. Dilip Kumar recalls working with him: 'I place him head and shoulders above his contemporaries because up to this day, I have not worked with any man with such all-round talent.' The one factor that most great directors have in common is their habit of working largely with a loyal team throughout their careers, and Bimal Roy was no exception.

> **Dharmesh Darshan**: When we work with the same team, we are bonded to those people. It's not that we don't enjoy working with a new unit, but we usually stick to the same people. Indians are highly emotional and India is essentially a place of relationships, and however professional we are, what we achieve in the films has a lot to do with the kind of people we are. We know the golden era of cinema is over. All the discoveries in cinema have already been made. We don't discover too many new things, we only discover technology. It's very unfortunate for us. Whatever we do now will echo something of the past and the best thing is not to feel ashamed about it, to accept the tradition they have set up for us, the legacy they have given us. Whether it's been Bimal Roy or Raj Kapoor, these filmmakers spoke to the heart. Raj Kapoor was a real master, he was an original.

Raj Kapoor's family has given Hindi cinema four generations of actors, from Prithviraj Kapoor to modern-day star Karishma Kapoor. The best-known member of the family in the West is Shashi Kapoor, who has starred in many international productions, working for Merchant-Ivory, among others. Raj Kapoor worked as a clapper boy with director Kidar Sharma, who famously gave him his first break as the hero in *Neel Kamal*

(1947). Kapoor was twenty-four when he directed his first film, 1948's *Aag*. It was followed a year later by *Barsaat*, a phenomenally successful love story about two couples, one of whom finds happiness, and the other, sorrow. A scene in *Barsaat* showing Nargis in Raj Kapoor's arms and a violin held in his other hand, symbolized the director's unique strengths – a mastery over romantic themes and a fine understanding of music – and indeed, throughout his career music and romance did go hand in hand. This striking image became the emblem for R.K. Films. Like Mehboob Khan, who knew how important the right environment was for creativity, Raj Kapoor built his own studio in 1950 – the R.K. Studios in Chembur, a western suburb of Bombay. The emblem above the entrance gates showing Nargis and Raj still welcomes all visitors today. R.K. Studios is still in use, and is now run by Raj Kapoor's eldest son, Randhir Kapoor, also an actor and director in his own right.

Raj Kapoor will always be remembered for his romanticism and lyricism. In *Barsaat*, the audience fell in love with the romantic pairing of (married) Raj Kapoor and his co-star, Nargis, and their romance on- and off-screen epitomized for many all that was sensuous and passionate. In 1951, Raj Kapoor released his most famous film, *Awaara* ('The Vagabond'), a story written by the celebrated left-wing author (and later filmmaker) K.A. Abbas and the journalist V.P. Sathe, both of whom were working as film critics at the *Bombay Chronicle* at the time. Initially, they had wanted Mehboob Khan to direct the film, but Mehboob had Dilip Kumar in mind for the role of Raju. Finally Raj Kapoor, hearing of the story, came to them, listened to the narration and took out a rupee from his pocket. V.P. Sathe remembers Raj Kapoor placing the rupee in Abbas's hand with the words: 'This story is mine.' When Raj Kapoor came to cast the film, he managed to persuade his father, Prithviraj, who had been a leading star since the 1930s, to play the hero's screen father, Judge Raghunath, and as expected, Kapoor cast Nargis to play Rita, a barrister and Judge Raghunath's ward.

Awaara is in many ways the perfect film – lighting, photography, brilliant storytelling, intelligent and witty dialogue, editing, music, strong performances, and romantic intensity are seamlessly blended together. The story of Raju and how he becomes a murderer is told in a series of flashbacks in the opening courtroom scene. Judge Raghunath is called to the dock and asked to explain his connection with the young criminal on trial. Raghunath denies any association with Raju, a man he considers a wastrel and vagabond. But Raghunath is forced by the defendant's lawyer, Rita, to delve into his own past. She persists: 'Under what circumstances, and why, did you throw your wife out of your home?' In the first of the many flashbacks, Raghunath recalls his past. Against social convention, he marries a widow, Leela, who is kidnapped by a bandit, Jagga (K.N. Singh). When Leela is finally returned to her husband, she is pregnant. Raghunath falls prey to gossip and throws Leela (played by Leela Chitnis) out of the house, suspecting her of carrying Jagga's child. In a fabulously orchestrated musical scene, Leela gives birth to Raju, the hero of the film, who is literally born in a city gutter. Raju (Raj Kapoor in his best performance) grows up groomed by the criminal Jagga who wants to prove to Raghunath, his old enemy, that good and bad character is not inborn but depends on upbringing. Years later, Raju, redeemed through Rita's love for him, is finally reunited with his father, Judge Raghunath, but Raju cannot escape punishment.

Awaara is also a love story told across two generations. Although Raghunath marries against convention, he cannot completely break with traditional thinking and is quick to suspect his wife of hiding the identity of her unborn child's father. He gives too much credence to the tongues that gossip *'Aap to jaante hi hain, sarkar, aurat ki zaat hi bewafaa hoti hain'* ('Master, you know well that all women are faithless'). The next generation of lovers, Raju and Rita, love each other in spite of Raju's criminal past and care little for what the world thinks.

The film started off as a moderate success in India, but made box-office history beyond the subcontinent. Raj Kapoor and Nargis became popular pin-ups in the Arab world; the film was dubbed into a number of languages in Russia, where it was much-loved; and the Chinese audience have never forgotten Raju and Rita. The songs, especially the title track, *'Awaara hun'*, were translated into several different languages and re-recorded and sung on the streets of all the countries in which the film was distributed.

Shree 420, which followed in 1955, was Raj Kapoor's other major film. This movie is Kapoor's tribute to his hero, Charlie Chaplin, and tells the story of the corrupting influence of Bombay on an idealistic young man called Raju who comes to the big city to make his fortune. In an interview in *Filmfare* in 1983, Kapoor talked about his admiration for Chaplin: 'What drew me to Chaplin's films was Chaplin himself. The hobo. The tramp. The common man. I was not drawn to him because of his get-up but because of his simplicity. The little man and the human emotions. How he enjoyed life even though he was so poor.' In *Shree 420*, the hero falls in love with the virtuous Vidya (Nargis) but is temporarily lured away by the vamp Maya

(Nadira). Naturally, the film ends happily, with Raju remembering his true values. The film features the most wonderful musical scenes, and the love duet 'Pyaar huaa ikraar huaa' ('We're in love and we know it') has the same uplifting and joyful mood captured in Gene Kelly's unforgettable title number from *Singin' in the Rain* (1952).

Nargis and Raj Kapoor split up in 1956, and their last film together was that year's *Jagte Raho*. Although Kapoor continued to make hugely successful movies, including *Sangam* (1964), which was his first film in colour and, like *Awaara*, a major hit with a non-Indian audience, and 1973's *Bobby*, his movies with Nargis have a magic that will always have a special place in the hearts of Hindi film fans. Raj Kapoor died on 2 June 1988, and his death marked the end of an era of filmmaking.

Manmohan Desai was the most interesting and innovative director of the 1970s. He brought energy and humour to the screen and added to the Amitabh Bachchan screen persona by making him a comic hero. Like the earlier directors, Manmohan Desai was an original and his films are now regarded among the classics of Hindi cinema. Desai allegedly committed suicide in 1994, and his death was a great loss both to the Indian film industry and to his many fans. Manmohan Desai saw Raj Kapoor as his idol and couldn't believe his luck when he managed to cast him in his first film, *Chhalia* (1960). In a television interview, Desai expressed fond memories of this early coup:

> **Manmohan Desai**: It was like a dream come true. I have been a great fan of Mr Raj Kapoor ever since childhood. I have seen all his films four or five times – *Awaara*, fourteen times. *Chhalia* had a very difficult theme, the

Partition theme. At that time, I didn't know much about scripting. I concentrated more on the action scenes and song visualizations. Making the film was a great experience. Though Raj Kapoor was a great director and actor, he never interfered in my work. He said, 'I'll do whatever you say.' And I made him act exactly as he would have acted in his own film *Awaara*. I had cast Nutan, whom I consider the all-time greatest actress that this country has ever seen. I was very fortunate to work with these two great actors.

The 1950s produced another of India's truly great film directors in the form of Guru Dutt. Guru Dutt was thirty-nine when he committed suicide on 10 October 1964 in Bombay. As he rightly suggested in his masterpiece *Pyaasa* (1957), an artist has greater value once he is dead – and with each decade since Guru Dutt's own death he has achieved even greater recognition. In March 2001, the Japan Foundation in Tokyo held a retrospective of Guru Dutt's films and they all played to a full house.

Guru Dutt Padukone was born in Bangalore on 9 July 1925 and when he was five years old his parents moved to Calcutta to work. Although he often went to the cinema, he did not think of a future in films because as a teenager he was more interested in dance. Thanks to the help of his uncle, B.B. Benegal, Guru Dutt won a scholarship to study dance at Uday Shankar's India Cultural Centre in Almora when he was seventeen. His training under Uday Shankar (Ravi Shankar's elder brother) was instrumental in forming his unique aesthetic sense. The influence of dance is evident in his editing pattern, and the way he uses camera movements – his tracking shots in particular have a ballet-like feel to them. When Uday Shankar's Centre closed down, Guru Dutt joined his family, who had moved from Calcutta to Bombay during the war years. Through the help of a family friend, Mr Pai, he joined the Prabhat Film Company in Pune as a choreographer, but also worked as an assistant director and even acted in a small role in Vishram Bedekar's *Lahkrani* (1945). In 1947, following India's Independence and Partition, Guru Dutt returned to Bombay and, because he spoke Bengali and was familiar with Bengali culture, he found work as an assistant to Amiya Chakravorty and Gyan Mukherjee.

In 1951, thanks to actor Dev Anand, whom he met at the Prabhat Film Company, Guru Dutt got his first break as director and made *Baazi*, a thriller involving a hero who is forced to turn to crime. This choice of theme was perhaps partly due to the influence of Gyan Mukherjee's famous *Kismet*, the first film to feature an anti-hero. *Baazi*, starring Dev Anand, Kalpana Kartik and Geeta Bali, is not one of Guru Dutt's classics, but is important because it brought new talent to the cinema. Balraj Sahni, who became a well-known actor and who was involved with IPTA (Indian People's Theatre Association), wrote the film's script. It was the second film by the exceptional music director S.D. Burman, and was one of the first of Urdu poet/lyricist Sahir Ludhianvi's movies.

During the making of *Baazi*, Guru Dutt met leading Bengali playback singer Geeta Roy, whom he married in 1953. Photographer V.K. Murthy, who became an essential member of the Guru Dutt team, also worked on *Baazi* (as a camera assistant), and later photographed all the key Guru Dutt films. Like Mehboob Khan, Bimal Roy and Raj Kapoor, Guru Dutt always believed in working with the same team; in later years, writer

Abrar Alvi, comedian Johnny Walker, Tun Tun and actress Waheeda Rahman became essential contributors to his work. V.K. Murthy describes one of Guru Dutt's strengths: 'He had a jeweller's eye. Just as a jeweller can find out which is the best diamond, he had the knack of extracting the best from a person.'

Guru Dutt's most-loved film is *Pyaasa*. It tells the story of Vijay (played by Dutt himself), an educated, middle-class poet. When Vijay's mother dies, his brothers throw him out to live on the streets where his friend, masseur Abdul Sattar (comedian Johnny Walker), has only his sense of humour to offer by way of support. A young prostitute named Gulab (the beautiful Waheeda Rahman) finds Vijay's poems and is struck by their sensitivity. A chance meeting brings them together, and Gulab falls in love with Vijay, although he is still emotionally tied to Meena (Mala Sinha). Meena is married to a successful publisher, Mr Ghosh, who can offer her a comfortable and secure life. Out of work and desperate, Vijay attempts suicide. When he is mistakenly believed to be dead, Gulab has his poetry published at her own expense. The book is an instant success and Vijay is lauded as a great poet. At a gathering held in his memory, Vijay returns from 'the dead' to decry the hypocrisy of the world around him.

Pyaasa is a powerful romantic melodrama telling of the thirst for love, for recognition and for values in a materialist society in which artists have no place. Guru Dutt transformed the character of Vijay in his next film, *Kaagaz ke Phool*, into film director Suresh Sinha, a successful middle-aged man whose personal life is in ruins. Estranged from his western-ized wife (Veena), he is denied access to his young daughter, Pammi (Baby Naaz). Suresh Sinha (played by Guru Dutt) discovers a young woman, Shanti (Waheeda Rahman), and makes her into a big star. They fall in love, but Pammi persuades Shanti to leave town, hoping that her parents might be reconciled. Years pass; Sinha has lost custody of his daughter, and his films are box-office disasters. He turns to drink, defeated by the cruel and superficial world of cinema in which he once stood supreme.

Kaagaz ke Phool was the first Indian film to be shot in Cinemascope and was exquisitely photographed in black and white by V.K. Murthy. It is Guru Dutt's tribute to the Bengali cinema of the 1930s and shows his fascination with the mechanics of filmmaking. After the success of *Pyaasa*, Dutt could never have imagined that *Kaagaz ke Phool*, his most personal film, would fail as miserably as it did at the box-office; his disillusionment was so great that he never signed another film as director, believing that to do so would bring the film bad luck. The similarities between Sinha's fortunes and Guru Dutt's own life-story led many to assume that the film was autobiographical. Guru Dutt's life, like Sinha's, showed an increasing split between the private and the public. Like Sinha, the adoration of his fans did nothing to lessen his sense of loneliness.

Guru Dutt felt the fullness of his work and the emptiness of his personal life acutely, in a divide between outer and inner reality that echoes the lives of many celebrities. In *Kaagaz ke Phool*, Suresh Sinha returns alone to his house from a star-studded premiere; he calls out to a servant, whom we do not see, '*Whisky laao*' ('Bring me some whisky'). His marriage was at its most turbulent at the time; like Sinha, he had become emotionally involved with his leading actress – Waheeda Rahman – whom he had discovered and who had become a star in her own right. Moreover, Sinha's death in anguish and solitude is prophetic of Guru Dutt's suicide five years later.

In 1962, Guru Dutt produced his next film, an adaptation of Bimal Mitra's Bengali novel, *Sahib Bibi aur Ghulam*, which is credited to his screenplay writer Abrar Alvi. This has caused a fair amount of controversy, as most of Guru Dutt's admirers cannot believe that Guru Dutt did not direct it himself. *Sahib Bibi aur Ghulam* is a magnificent and sombre work with remarkable performances, rich dialogues and heightened atmosphere. Ironically, it was the only Guru Dutt film to win a *Filmfare* Best Director award, which went to Abrar Alvi in 1962; while Guru Dutt himself (as producer) collected *Filmfare*'s award for Best Film.

During the making of his last film in 1964, *Baharen Phir Bhi Ayenge* ('The Spring will Return', directed by Shaheed Latif), finally released in 1966, Guru Dutt was living alone in a rented apartment, separated from his wife Geeta and their three children, Tarun, Arun and Neena. His relationship with Waheeda Rahman had come to an end during the making of *Sahib Bibi aur Ghulam*. To his colleagues, Guru Dutt seemed to be in good health and engrossed in making the film. Raj Kapoor had arranged to meet Guru Dutt on 10 October, and was shocked to find his friend had committed suicide during the previous night.

Working within a cinema dominated largely by formula, Guru Dutt transformed repetitive ingredients into a poetic and personal vision. His relationship with the Indian and worldwide audience remains a special one. Unlike the films of Mehboob Khan and Raj Kapoor, which spawned many clones, Guru Dutt's movies did not feed the formula, as they were so deeply personal and so connected to his vision of the world. He mastered all the conventions of Hindi cinema: his musical sequences stand out for their simple and effective moods; he achieved a fine balance between the main plot and the various subplots; his approach to photography and lighting was unusual in that he made them work for him as another character.

Guru Dutt is at his subtlest in the characterization of his heroes and heroines, who are, pyschologically speaking, the most interesting characters in Hindi cinema. He proved how little emotional drama was necesssary in a film if the audience was already engaged internally with a character. A single shot in *Pyaasa*, showing Gulab standing at the top of the stairs over-whelmed with emotion that Vijay has at last come to her, is just one of the indelible images to be found in his work. Guru Dutt's films quietly yet assuredly demonstrate why cinema has become the most powerful medium of our time. Dharmesh Darshan acknowledges that, 'Guru Dutt is a God for me. Raj Kapoor and Guru Dutt's work excites me. Their films were conventional Indian cinema, yet so unconventional.'

The division in India between popular and New Cinema was blurred in the 1950s, when these gifted directors managed to make meaningful and individual films within the framework of popular cinema. By the 1970s, Hindi cinema had become increasingly dependent on the formula film and some of the New Cinema directors who were prominent in that decade were outspoken in their criticism and rejection of it.

New Cinema productions had hoped to find a large audience in India, but these films did not appeal to the masses, who stuck to the formula film. Until the mid-eighties, much of Hindi cinema suffered from a negative reputation, even within India; Bombay productions were largely dismissed as populist and mindless rubbish. Since then, however, Hindi cinema has been

the subject of reappraisal, and film critics and scholars throughout the world have shown a keen interest in the conventions of
this unique branch of filmmaking. Indian film directors and
Hindi films are now the subject of academic studies, and the
number of biographies on filmmakers and general books on
Indian cinema is on the increase. That said, Hindi films are still
on the margins of world culture and while the world of
Bollywood intrigues the press in the West, many film directors of
the Indian popular cinema are still scarcely known there.

Since the 1980s, Bollywood budgets have increased vastly,
and so predictability and repetition have become even more
important. Sanjay Leela Bhansali, who is one of the most gifted
directors today, is extremely conscious of how hard it is for a
director to recover the costs of a film:

Sanjay Leela Bhansali: Whenever you come up with an
interesting storyline, the producers or the financiers will
say, 'This won't run'. So you have to think within a
formula – and your thinking is restricted. You have to be
a very strong person to compromise on the storyline,
because what *you* may want to make won't work. In an
Indian cinema, the audience is very different from one
section to the other, financially, economically and
socially; completely different temperamentally. If I have
to pack in everything in a single film and have to keep
them happy, it means I have to use less of my own
instincts and brains. And when I'm writing the film, I
have to think about what they will like. And they may not
like my kind of story. The producers will back out too
because the audience finally make the film a hit or a flop.

You have to stick to the formula. You cannot develop your ideas. You can't talk about new things – people have done it, but it requires a lot of guts. A director here has to be strong, a little bit sensitive, a little insensitive, shameless, and yet sometimes true. You have to be a complete filmmaker. You have to have as much grasp on music and dance as on costumes, as on the values in my grandmother's times – not of the values of my time, not of what I believe is right and wrong. So there's a lot of demand on an Indian filmmaker, constant pressure, it's tremendous. Sometimes it's killing, sometimes when the film works, it's a great high. But I'm sure if Steven Spielberg was asked to make a Hindi film, he'd run away.

How does an aspiring filmmaker get started in Bollywood today? As in most film industries in the world, young directors start off by assisting other directors on as many movies as they can, and then desperately try to get finance for their first film. The other option for a newcomer is to join the Film Institute of India (known as the FTII), which is based in Pune in the old studios of the Prabhat Film Company. FTII students have a great advantage in having access to the National Film Archives, a five-minute walk away, which organizes regular screenings of world classics. One of the1990s' biggest directors, David Dhawan, graduated as a film editor at the FTII. It took him eleven years to make the transition from editor to director, and he now makes blockbuster movies, many in tandem with the star Govinda. Inspired by the energetic and unusual Manmohan Desai, David Dhawan has developed a style of his own. His films are very much like fairy tales, in which the poor village lad nearly always marries the rich princess and lives happily ever after. His *Raja Babu* is particularly hilarious in its depiction of the ways in which mothers spoil their sons silly.

David Dhawan: Way back in the 1970s, my brother, Anil Dhawan, joined the Film Institute and became an actor, so I joined as well, to train as an editor. We'd see such lovely films there. I saw *Meghe Dhaka Tara* by Ritwik Ghatak, a Bengali film, no subtitles, nothing, I didn't know anything about it. I just walked into the theatre, I thought I'd sit for half an hour and go. I couldn't get up. I was crying at the end of the film. It took me two days to get over that film. A low-budget film, but what a soundtrack Ghatak had created. It had an amazing story but the narrative was so simple. It's a great film. I still remember it.

I graduated from the Film Institute as a gold medallist in 1976. It was a major problem coming from there and fitting into the Bombay film industry. They didn't welcome me. When I'd get to work, they used to say, 'Ah, this film institute boy has come.' They treated me like a student – 'what can this learned guy teach us?' Breaking the ice wasn't easy. I got a job in Bombay television and worked as an editor. I used to get about 700 rupees a month [£10]. I edited documentaries for *Unicef* and some ad films. And in 1977, I got my first feature film to edit, it was called *Saajan Bina Sauhagan*, with Nutanji and Rajendra Kumar. I edited about fifty feature films. That's how I got into direction in 1987. The transition wasn't very difficult. If you know how to edit a film, it makes things easier. I knew I'd need a shot here, a shot there. So I don't waste time. And I know exactly what I want – where I need a close-up, a long shot and trolley. So I don't take hours to shoot and the actors are happier.

Today's A-list directors, including Mahesh Bhatt, J.P. Dutta, Rajkumar Santoshi, Inder Kumar and Rakesh Roshan, have an easier time dealing with the star system, as their names are equally important in selling the film. The same is true of some of the top producers such as Boney Kapoor, Yash Chopra and Subhash Ghai (Chopra and Ghai are also extremely successful directors), all of whom have a lot of clout in the industry. The old guard of filmmakers tend to go for the big canvas film that often follows a transparent trajectory respecting every formulaic convention of the Bollywood mix including music, action, romance and, of course, a moral tale as the integral theme.

Mani Ratnam is one of the most interesting directors working in Indian popular film today. He works principally in Tamil cinema and has made highly successful films. Hindi versions of *Roja* (1992) and *Bombay* (1994) did excellent business, as did his Hindi film, *Dil Se* (1998). Like the old masters, Mani Ratnam has managed to make meaningful and lyrical films while working within Hindi cinema conventions.

Mani Ratnam: I have chosen to work within the mainstream. I am trying to make films that I want people to see. I have to talk in a language that is understood. I don't think you should look at the conventions of Hindi cinema as constraints. If you start doing that, you are shying away from them. It is the way we tell our stories, the way we tell our films. So make the films to the best of your ability and add your sensibilities. Regarding repetition, I don't know whether this is unique to film-making in India. It's the same all over the world. Somebody makes a James Bond film, and then there's Bond after Bond. I pity the guy who has to write the script again and again.

In recent films, directors have tried to counter-balance repetition by introducing an interesting new twist in storytelling. This new twist involves a short-hand form – relying on a line of dialogue, or a simple explanation, that will evoke in the minds of the audience established scenes from previous movies. In Subhash Ghai's *Taal* (1999), Anil Kapoor's character has the line, 'Like the Hindi film hero, abandoned by his father, my mother raised me by doing menial sewing jobs.' It's now sufficient for Anil Kapoor to speak of his struggling past, rather than *Taal* requiring scenes that actually show this struggle. To move the narrative along, many directors today rely on the familiarity of formula that has been mastered equally by filmmaker and audience.

The golden age of Indian cinema may have passed, but the films produced during that time continue to work their magic on successive generations of audiences and directors. And film-makers today are still learning from them. Dharmesh Darshan believes that the achievements of Mehboob Khan, Bimal Roy, Raj Kapoor and Guru Dutt were due in part to the challenges they faced, and argues that such struggles are essential in developing a filmmaker's creativity:

Dharmesh Darshan: One very big drawback my generation of filmmakers and actors have is that they have not struggled in life. Everything is instant, the food and the success. In the past, they really struggled – the writers, the filmmakers – they took years to make it in films. Even in the old days in Hollywood, directors would sometimes be forty or forty-five years old when they made their first film. First they would be clapper boys, canteen boys, assistant editors, then editors, assistant directors and finally, directors. The struggle has really gone; however, please don't assume that there's no personal struggle. I think the difference is that in the past people used to struggle before making it, today people struggle after making it [*laughs*].

But the earlier directors had longevity. Once a director made it, he lasted thirty or forty years. Today, the ones who make it very quickly also risk disappearing quickly. Today, actors don't suffer from inner turmoil. And that takes away from the magic. The magic of creativity lies in the struggle for survival; in the past, if you weren't diligent, you'd be on the streets. Filmmakers and stars today have a full stomach. Everyone is pretty happy, secure, everyone has major bank accounts, everyone speaks articulately and is well read. But if I couldn't make films, I wouldn't survive. I live and thrive on cinema. And, of course, I'm smart enough to make a living out of it.

Chapter Seven

SINGING THROUGH THE AGES

Indian films are totally dependent on music. Indian audiences tolerate repeated film plots, and accept the same characters, sometimes even saying the same things, but they expect Indian film music to demonstrate originality. Even though the tunes are often 'lifted' – in every decade, a music director is accused of copying a Western pop or rock number, or an Egyptian or African melody – no song featuring in one film can be used again in another. If there is cross-referencing with other songs, this takes places in the form of an *antakshari*. This is the name of a musical game played in north India that involves two rival groups, or individuals, who sing the catch line (*mukhra*) of a song. When the first singer stops, the next player starts singing a catch line from a different song that must begin with the last letter of the previous *mukhra*. This musical quiz game also reveals how many millions of people in India know hundreds of film songs by heart. *Antakshari* sequences have always been popular in Hindi films, and even more so on television. As David Page and William Crawley note in *Satellites Over South Asia*, 'Since satellite television ended Doordarshan's [state-run television] monopoly, talent-spotting competitions and shows encouraging audience participation, like *Meri Awaz Suno*, *Antakshari* and *Sa Re Ga Ma*, have developed very large audiences all over India, especially among the young' (*Satellites Over South Asia*, Sage Publications, New Delhi/Thousand Oaks/London, 2001). For that matter, no form of entertainment in India, traditional or contemporary, exists without some kind of musical accompaniment.

> **Karan Johar**: Everyone in the West asks why every Indian film is a musical – it's simply because music is a great part of our culture. We are very firmly rooted as a country, as people of India, and music is so much part of us, it is so much part of our heritage, of our religion. Every religious festival, there are songs that are sung. In our day-to-day living, we wake up to music, we sleep to music. We live for music. So therefore it has to be in our films.

Almost every festive event or private occasion for celebration, such as childbirth or marriage, is accompanied by its own music. All religions and rituals have their own compositions, such as the Hindu devotional *bhajan* (or *kirtan*), and the Muslim *qawwali*, the Sufi music of India and Pakistan usually performed by professional male singers at the shrines of Sufi saints. Each regional area from Kashmir to Kanya Kumari has a long and rich tradition of folk music. The conventions of classical and folk theatre include drama, music, song and dance. Consequently, in 1931, when Ardeshir Irani made *Alam Ara*, India's first sound film, with composer Ferozshah M. Mistri, he borrowed the basic structure from the plays of the Parsee Theatre, which featured a number of songs based on Hindustani light-classical music. In their use of musical interludes, songs and dances, the early talkies created a new and distinct genre of Indian music – that of the film song. After the success of these early song-filled movies, music became an essential component, featuring in all popular cinema. Today, music is recognized as compensating for frequently weak, formulaic scripts, and for providing the glue that binds the audience to Hindi cinema. Film songs follow set patterns, as lyricist Javed Akhtar points out:

Javed Akhtar: These days an Indian film has five or six songs, whether it is a war movie, a romantic film, a family drama or whatever the genre may be. The menu is fixed. And so we have some set situations in which we have songs. As lyricists, we have to write songs again and again and again for similar kinds of situations. For example, when the boy is wooing the girl, or when the girl is announcing her love for the boy, or they are in love, they sing a duet, or they are separated and sing a song pining for each other. These are the main romantic situations for a song. Besides romance, you have cabaret songs, lullabies, occasionally patriotic or nationalist songs, devotional songs like the *bhajan* or the *qawwali*. But the list is not too long!

An Indian recording industry producing commercial recordings had started in 1902, some years before the first home-grown films were produced. These recordings mainly consisted of *ghazals* and *qawwalis*. The *ghazals* were particularly appreciated by middle-class, educated north Indians who spoke both Hindi and Urdu. G.N. Joshi, a 1930s lyric singer and recording executive at the British-owned Gramophone Company of India (by 1920, GCI traded under the HMV label, 'His Master's Voice'), describes the impact of the early recordings: 'At the end of the record and the close of the singing, each artist was required to announce his or her name in English, [as in] "My name is Janakibai of Allahabad", or "My name is Mushtaribai of Agra." These announcements in English by performers who did not know the English language at all, amused the listeners and helped to boost the sale of records' ('A concise history of the phonography industry in India' in *Popular Music*, Vol 7 No 2, Cambridge University Press, 1988). By the mid-1930s, when HMV started to market the soundtracks of Hindustani films, this music with its all-India character very quickly overshadowed the sales of stage songs, regional folk music and classical music recordings. Before long, film music had become *the* popular music of the Indian subcontinent.

Technical limitations played a large part in determining how a song would look in the early films. Recordings were made on film negative in synch sound, and this procedure greatly limited the visual potential of the early song. A single microphone was fixed on a stand and directed at the actor/singer while a small number of musicians (sarangi player, tabla player and harmonium player – the same ensemble that performed during the silent era) sat behind the camera. The constraining setting meant that the actor could not move very much for fear of upsetting the sound balance between his voice and the musical backing. The camera, too, could not move or pan, and so the song would be filmed in an extended static take. Live recordings also necessitated the use of blankets and mattresses to muffle camera noise; furthermore, the studios were not soundproof (the majority of studio floors are still not soundproof even today). Early sound recordists remember with amusement that the cawing of crows could sometimes be heard among the voices of the singing chorus. Film historian P.K. Nair dates early dubbing techniques to the mid-1930s, when songs were no longer recorded live during the take. Instead, the actor would pre-record a song and this would be played back on set as actors moved or danced while lip-synching to their own voices.

The success of *Alam Ara* and its famous songs showed that music was a great crowd-puller. An early record-breaker was 1932's *Indarsabha* (J.F. Madan; composer Nagardas Nayak) based on Nawab Wajid Ali Shah's play of the same name and starring Nissar, Jehanara, Kajjan and Mukhtar Begum (also a composer). *Indarsabha*'s romantic narrative featured many subplots; it was written in fine Urdu verse and boasted of having seventy-one songs. Interestingly, the use of playback singing did not come until 1935, with Nitin Bose's film *Dhoop Chhaon* (composers Rai Chand Boral and Pankaj Mullick), which was said to be the first movie to employ such a technique.

After sound came to Hollywood in 1927 with *The Jazz Singer*, American cinema moved away from using songs in all film genres, creating instead a separate cinematic genre: the musical. In contrast, all genres of Indian film continue to feature songs to this day, and any attempt by popular cinema to exclude them has led to box-office disaster. One such example is the 1937 film *Naujawan*. Despite the fact that producer J.B.H. Wadia explained the absence of songs in a trailer shown before the film, *Naujawan* failed to appeal. The songless *Munna* (1954, K.A. Abbas) and *Kanoon* (1960, B.R. Chopra) also suffered a similar fate (despite the fact that *Kanoon* won its director a *Filmfare* award). And so it became a prerequisite for the 1930s stars to have a good singing voice.

> **P.K. Nair:** Indian filmmakers realized that sound was a very interesting way of introducing songs in films, along with the spoken dialogue. So we have singing stars right from the beginning of the talkies. Famous actresses of the time could sing, including Zubeida, Durga Khote, Shanta Apte and Kanan Devi. There was also Pankaj Mullick, who was a music director as well as a singer and actor. And K.C. Dey [playback singer Manna Dey's uncle] was a famous blind singer at the New Theatres in Calcutta and sang the song, *'Mat bhool musafir'* ['O traveller, do not forget'] in *Devdas*. Then in Bombay, we had Surendranath, Khurshid and many other singing stars. The most popular was undoubtedly Kundanlal Saigal. He was a good singer and because of that, screenplays were written primarily to give scope to his singing talent.

Kundanlal (or K.L. as he was popularly known) Saigal was a star performer who inspired hysterical adulation. K.L. Saigal was born in Jullunder, Punjab, in 1904. He dropped out of school and worked in Calcutta as a typewriter salesman. Saigal dreamed of joining the movies and the dream came true when B.N. Sircar, the owner of New Theatres, put him on the studio payroll. The music directors R.C. Boral and Pankaj Mullick were Saigal's early mentors and his first success came with *Chandidas* (1934, Nitin Bose; composer R.C. Boral). The studios also employed another excellent music composer who was trained in classical music, Timir Baran, who was a disciple of the sarod masters Amir Khan and Allauddin Khan. In 1935, while R.C. Boral was composing the music for the Bengali version of *Devdas*, Timir Baran wrote the music for its Hindi version, which was being filmed simultane-ously. The Hindi songs featured in *Devdas*, sung by Saigal and including '*Balam ayo baso mere man mein*' ('O beloved, come into my heart'), were phenomenally successful and gave the New Theatres an edge over the other studios in the area of music. In his article 'In Eternal Quest of the New', Arun Chattopadhyay quotes the celebrated music director Naushad on the impact that the New Theatres had on film songs: 'In the early stages, film music was not popular. The credit for popularizing film music goes to the New Theatres of Calcutta. They introduced the orchestra in film songs, and since then, orchestration has spread through the film world.' (*Cinema Vision*, Vol iii No 11)

K.L. Saigal sang in a low pitch, and specialized in the singing of *ghazals* (Urdu lyric poems set to music), a form that featured just a few musical instruments such as the tabla, tanpura and harmonium. His singing style showed a wide range and the soft quality of his voice helped to establish a new style of popular singing. He is also remembered for being the first singer to give the right stress to the lyrics, and so his renditions of the work of Urdu poet Ghalib remain exemplary to this day. Filmmaker and critic Partha Chatterjee aptly sums up Saigal's talent thus:

'Though not trained in classical music, he knew the structure and nuances of ragas by instinct, and could render complex forms of light-classical music like *ghazal*, *thumri*, and *bhajan* with an unequalled sense of truth.' ('When Melody Ruled the Day', *Indian Horizons*, Vol 44, Indian Council for Cultural Relations, Delhi)

In 1941, K.L. Saigal left for Bombay to work for Ranjit Studios, whose production of *Tansen* (1943, Jayant Desai; composer Khemchand Prakash) was particularly successful. Saigal's last film, *Shahjehan* (1946, A.R. Kardar; composer Naushad), featured some of his most beautiful and melancholic songs, written by Majrooh Sultanpuri, including '*Gham diye mustakil, itna nazuk hai dil ye na jaana*' ('The inflicted sorrow is absolute, I never knew how fragile is the heart') and '*Jab dil hi toot gaya, hum ji ke kya karenge*' ('When my heart is broken, what use is living?'). K.L. Saigal was perhaps the first superstar of Indian cinema, but despite his incredible success – and like the hero Devdas he was to immortalize – he became an alcoholic and died of cirrhosis of the liver at the age of forty-two in 1946. The singer C.H. Atma later attempted to emulate his style, but Saigal proved irreplaceable.

There were a number of important female singing stars in the 1940s, but Noorjehan and Suraiya made the biggest impression. In 1948 and 1949, Suraiya had three major hits: *Pyar Ki Jeet* (O.P. Dutta; composers Husnlal-Bhagatram), *Badi Behan* (D.D. Kashyap; composers Husnlal-Bhagatram), and *Dilliagi* (A.R. Kardar; composer Naushad). She was also cast in a love triangle story by Mehboob Khan (*Anmol Ghadi*, 1946, composer Naushad), which also featured Noorjehan and Surendranath. However, by the mid-1950s, Suraiya had virtually retired from film; her last appearance came in 1963's *Rustom Sohrab* (Vishram Bedekar, composer Sajjad Hussain). Today, Suraiya lives a reclusive life in Bombay.

One of the most important singing stars, Noorjehan was introduced to film by director K.D. Mehra in the studios of pre-independence Lahore. Her first success came with Dalsukh Pancholi's 1942 film *Khandaan* (composer Ghulam Haider), directed by her first husband Shaukat Hussain Rizvi. Noorjehan moved to Bombay in the 1940s, where her star charisma and excellent singing won her the best roles on offer. Her most fondly remembered song of this period featured in Mehboob's *Anmol Ghadi* and was a romantic duet with singing star Surendranath – '*Awaaz de kahan hai, duniya meri jawan hai*' ('Call out to me, where are you now? My world is young'). In 1947, Noorjehan migrated to Pakistan. She continued working there as a leading actress in Pakistani cinema and became a much-fêted singer and personality, known as the Queen of Melody. Noorjehan lived an unconventional life, divorcing Rizvi when she was forty, and marrying a younger man. She died in December 2000, by which time she had become well established as an icon of song.

In the mid-1930s, the practice of 'playback singing' (as opposed to the earlier dubbing techniques in which an actor would lip-synch to his own voice) was introduced in India. Even today, film songs are entirely dependent on this 'invisible' contribution by a singing talent. Playback singing involves a singer recording a song that is then 'played back' on location. The actor on whom the song is picturized mimes to the words as the song is filmed. Once the playback singers arrived on the scene, thereby freeing the screen talent from the need to be able to sing themselves, the casting net widened and a new group of stars emerged, approaching film acting in quite a different way from the stage actors of previous years. The playback technique enabled stars including Dilip Kumar, Raj Kapoor, Dev Anand, Nargis, Meena Kumari and Madhubala to confidently build their careers, no longer afraid of being let down by a weak singing voice.

No records exist of the very first song recorded by a playback singer. One early recording is said to have been made by India's first female music director, Saraswati Devi. A Parsee, Saraswati Devi was forced to change her name from Khorshed Minochar-Homji to avoid the anger of her community when she and her sister, Manek, joined Bombay Talkies. But her songs were to enable Bombay Talkies to make a mark on the film music scene. Saraswati Devi proved to be a talented composer, and her first major success came at the age of twenty-four, with *Achhut Kanya* (1936, Franz Osten). One song from the film, '*Main ban ki chidiya ban ban*' (sung by Ashok Kumar and Devika Rani), became famous and is still loved for its simple and direct charm. Saraswati Devi had been a champion of classical music and stopped composing for films in 1950, by which time the musical influences in cinema had changed substantially.

The 1930s playback singers included Amirbai Karnataki, Zohrabai and Mubarak Begum. These singers sang in a more *mehfil* style – a style associated with a song recital usually meant for a small gathering of people, in which the microphone was seldom, if ever, used. Other early playback singers included Rajkumari, Juthika Ray, Kamal Das Gupta, Durrani, Meena Kapur (music director Anil Biswas' wife) and in later years, Sudha Malhotra. The wonderful Shamshad Begum was another early playback singer who, like Lata Mangeshkar, owed her entry into films to music director Ghulam Haider. Shamshad Begum continued singing into the 1950s, specializing in folky, earthy songs.

By the mid-1930s, with the active encouragement of the famous Bengali composer Anil Biswas, more and more artists began to sing for screen actors. In the early days of playback singing, film producers did not advertise the fact that their actors were singing in a borrowed voice. The most famous playback singer ever, Lata Mangeshkar, who recorded the stunning, melodious 'Aayega aanewala' for Kamaal Amrohi's 1949 film *Mahal* (composer Khemchand Prakash), found that her name did not feature on the 78rpm disc, as she remembers:

Lata Mangeshkar: If you see the original record, the name of the singer credited is 'Kamini', the name of the character Madhubala plays in the film. I remember thousands of letters were sent to All India Radio requesting that this song be played. The listeners also wanted to know who sang the song. So the All India Radio presenter called the producer of *Mahal* and then it was announced on the radio that 'Aayega aanewala' was sung by Lata Mangeshkar. But I had to fight for us playback singers to be credited and the first film in which our names featured on screen is Raj Kapoor's 1949 film *Barsaat*.

Lata Mangeshkar is said to have sung over 25,000 songs since she began lending her voice to the screen in *Majboor* (Nazir Ajmeri, composer Ghulam Haider) in 1948. She is officially the world's most recorded singer, an achievement that has earned

her a place in the *Guinness Book of Records*. She began learning music at the age of five with her father Dinanath
Mangeshkar, and every subsequent teacher who taught her
immediately recognized her genius. There was apparently no
song or *raag* that young Lata could not master effortlessly.
When her father died, Lata Mangeshkar had to help provide for
the family and acted in Marathi films as a child artist. She wasn't
keen on acting and was relieved when she found that instead she
could earn a living by singing for the cinema. One of her special
gifts is the stress she gives to every word she sings, bringing out
the finest shades of expression in Hindi and Urdu, and the many
languages in which she can sing with equal ease. She has sung
for all the best actresses and if we are moved by Nargis's songs
in *Mother India* or Nutan's simplicity in *Seema*, or Preity Zinta's
charm in *Dil Se*, the credit goes to Lata Mangeshkar, whose
talent is vital to the overall impact of an actress's performance.
Today's newcomers only believe they have made it, if Lata
Mangeshkar agrees to sing for them.

Removing her shoes before she enters a recording studio as
a sign of respect (as one would in a temple or place of worship),
Lata Mangeshkar first hears the tune of a song, usually sung by
the music director, reads through the lyrics and marks the text at
points where she will pause, or give stress to a particular word.
She rehearses the song once and then in one, at most two takes,
the song is recorded. In the 1950s, Lata Mangeshkar would
record four songs a day. She has won India's highest honour, the
Bharat Ratna, and the greatest number of awards imaginable,
not only for her exceptional catalogue of songs, which spans five
decades, but also because she has earned the love of the nation.
She is the most respected woman in the Indian film industry and

is an enduring icon loved without reservation in India, Pakistan, Bangladesh and in the Diaspora. Lata Mangeshkar has a tinkling laugh and an intelligent and analytical mind. She is a musician's singer, but despite the amazing adulation she has received throughout her life, she remains pious, humble and private.

Lata Mangeshkar: I receive many letters. People write wanting to meet me. They say, 'We want to pay our respects to you.' The love that I have received is a great thing. No one has ever said, 'When we hear you sing, we feel like hitting you.' But receiving people's love is the most important thing in life. Who could imagine I would be so famous? All right, I can sing. But it isn't anything extraordinary. Many have sung better than me but they didn't get as much in life. Whatever we have is because of His benevolence, whatever you choose to call Him – Allah, Ishwar or Jesus Christ. I always pray in the morning and at night before I sleep. I am very grateful to God that my success has not had a detrimental effect on me. My head could have turned. I could have thought no end of myself. But I consider myself nothing. Whatever has happened has been His will. And if He believes it should not be so, in a minute, all this can turn to dust.

A small number of playback singers, who started their career in the late 1940s, including Lata Mangeshkar, proved to be so gifted that they dominated the next few decades of Hindi film music. The leading male singers were Mohammed Rafi, Mukesh, Kishore Kumar, Talat Mahmood and Manna Dey, while Lata Mangeshkar, her younger sister Asha Bhosle, and Geeta

Dutt (Guru Dutt's wife) were the leading female artists. Between them, Lata Mangeshkar, Mohammed Rafi, Asha Bhosle, Mukesh and Kishore Kumar have sung the lion's share of the songs in films since the 1940s. Their solos and duets have encapsulated the love lives of millions of people, for whom they defined the concept of romance and the complexity of emotions.

The actor Motilal helped the young Mukesh to get into films. Mukesh had always wanted to be an actor rather than a singer, but he didn't make a successful hero. His début as a singer came in *Pahali Nazar* (1945, Mazhar Khan; composer Anil Biswas) in the song *'Dil jalta hai to jalne de'* ('If my heart burns, let it burn'). The song was a big success, although Mukesh was criticized for imitating Saigal's singing style. Mehboob Khan's films *Anokhi Ada* (1948) and the following year's *Andaaz*, both of which featured music by composer Naushad, gave Mukesh the songs that he needed to show the distinctive attraction and depth of his voice. In *Andaaz*, his heartfelt melodies, *'Tu kahe agar'* ('If you tell me') and *'Toote na dil toote na'* ('May my heart never be broken'), added greatly to the pathos of the rejected lover, played by Dilip Kumar. Starting with *Awaara* (1951), Mukesh began to sing for Raj Kapoor, an association that was to prove so successful that Mukesh's voice still evokes an image of Raj Kapoor in the minds of listeners. One of the most famous songs of Hindi cinema, *'Mera Joota hai Japani'* ('My shoes are Japanese') from *Shree 420*, shows Raj Kapoor heading off from a village to Bombay, 420 miles away. This Mukesh song has helped to render Raj Kapoor's hero timeless. Mukesh died in 1976 of a heart attack while on a concert tour of the USA with Lata Mangeshkar. On hearing of his friend's death, Raj Kapoor said simply, 'My soul has died.'

From the early 1950s, associating a singer and a hero became a tradition in film music. The audience completely accepted this division of talent and are still happy to see Shahrukh Khan miming to Sukhwinder Singh's voice or accept Kavita Krishnamurthy singing for Aishwarya Rai. Kavita Krishnamurthy believes that, 'Indians are used to the concept of playback singing and they would rather have a beautiful song on screen from a beautiful woman than have a beautiful woman singing in a very bad voice.' A superb parody of playback singing features in *Padosan* (1968, Jyoti Swaroop; composer R.D. Burman). We see the hero (Sunil Dutt) wooing his neighbour (Saira Banu) with the song, *'Mere saamnevali khirki main ek chand sa tukra rehta hai'* ('In front of my window lives a piece of the moon'), sung by his buddy (played by Kishore Kumar), who is standing out of sight of the pretty heroine, gesticulating furiously.

Another important playback singer was Talat Mahmood, whose soulful vibrato style was particularly suited to the *ghazal*. As long as Indian film music had a base in Indian tradition, Talat Mahmood remained popular. However, unlike other singers, Mahmood's voice did not suit the westernized melodies that began influencing film music, and by the late 1950s he was recording less and less. His voice had a softness and sensitivity that always made it particularly effective at creating a romantic mood. Talat Mahmood, Hemant Kumar (who is also a brilliant music director), and Geeta Dutt were exceptionally effective at suggesting a soulful and mesmerizing mood in many black and white classics. It comes as no surprise to learn that S.D. Burman, who introduced Geeta Dutt to film music, had considered using Talat Mahmood as his main singer at one point. S.D.

Burman also hired Hemant Kumar to sing in many of his compositions. Talat Mahmood's *Jayen to jayen kahaan* picturized on Dev Anand in *Taxi Driver* (1954, Chetan Anand; composer S.D. Burman), Geeta Dutt's *Kahin door se awaaz de* picturized on Meena Kumari in *Sahib Bibi aur Ghulam* (1961, Abrar Alvi; composer Hemant Kumar), and Hemant Kumar's *Ye raat ye chandni phir kahaan* picturized on Dev Anand in *Jaal* (1952, Guru Dutt; composer S.D. Burman) are filled with emotional yearning and melancholy. The impact of these songs on audiences today is just as powerful as when they were first heard.

The only person to have combined a successful career as both actor and playback singer was the Bengali Kishore Kumar. He had an exuberant style, even adding yodelling to his considerable range. The younger brother of the star Ashok Kumar, Kishore Kumar was one of the best comedians of Indian cinema. *Chalti Ka Naam Gaadi* (1958, Satyen Bose; composer S.D. Burman), *Half Ticket* (1962, Kalidas; composer Salil Choudhury) and *Aasha* (1957, M.V. Raman; composer C. Ramachandra) are examples of his unique brand of humour, a reckless and subtle mix of surrealism and madcap comedy. His second marriage, to the gorgeous Madhubala, came as a big surprise, as it was assumed that she would marry Dilip Kumar. By the end of the 1950s, Kishore Kumar was hardly making any films as an actor, choosing to make playback singing his main profession. He sang for all the top stars, starting with Dev Anand in *Ziddi* (1948, Shaheed Latif; composer Khemchand Prakash) through to Amitabh Bachchan in 1977's *Amar Akbar Anthony* (Manmohan Desai, composers Laxmikant-Pyarelal). During the 1970s, Kishore Kumar was the most popular male singer, and the highest paid. His voice was melodic and full of character, and he was particularly adept at adding a touch of mischief and fun to his comic songs and a hint of romantic seduction to his sexy numbers. Kishore Kumar died in October 1987, leaving behind thousands of songs as testament to his enormous talent.

In the history of Indian film music, however, there is no other male singer who has had, and continues to have, as many devoted fans as the gifted Mohammed Rafi, who died in 1980. When Rafi died, there followed a ten-year period in which every new male singer was compared to him and invariably found wanting. Not a day passes without a Rafi song being broadcast on the hundreds of radio or television stations on the Indian sub-continent and in the Diaspora. Mohammed Rafi, a devout Muslim who never drank or smoked, became the voice of Hindustan, and from 1950 to 1969, every star wanted him to sing for them. He embraced every musical mood and sang poignant *ghazals* for Dev Anand, classical songs for Dilip Kumar or Bharat Bhushan, rock 'n' roll numbers for Shammi Kapoor, gentle love songs for Guru Dutt, Rajendra Kumar, Dharmendra or Raaj Kumar, cheeky comic songs for Johnny Walker, and *qawwalis* for Rishi Kapoor with equal ease.

Mohammed Rafi was born in the village of Kotta Sultan Singh (now part of Pakistan) on 4 December 1924. A move to Lahore in 1938 saw him study music with Ghulam Ali Khan, Jeevanlal Matto and Khan Abdul Waheed Khan. He began his career by performing on Radio Lahore before his first film, the Punjabi *Gul Baloch* (composer Shyam Sunder) in 1944. His only memorable song from the 1940s was a love duet with Noorjehan, '*Yahan badla wafaa ka*' in *Jugnu* (1947, Shaukat Hussain Rizvi; composer Feroze Nizami). It was rumoured that Naushad was angry with Talat Mahmood for smoking in his presence and called Rafi instead to sing his compositions for *Baiju Bawra* (1952, Vijay Bhatt). Mohammed Rafi's renditions of Naushad's classical music-based songs in the film and the sweet romantic melodies featured in *Aan* convinced other composers of his rare singing ability. His voice, like Lata Mangeshkar's, added greatly to the performances of actors, and if Dilip Kumar or Balraj Sahni have moved audiences, it is in part because of the expression that Rafi gave to their songs.

In the 1970s, Mohammed Rafi was superseded by Kishore Kumar, but for many he remains Indian cinema's most talented playback singer. The most vivacious actor of the 1960s, Shammi Kapoor, is still moved when he thinks of this versatile and exceptional singer:

Shammi Kapoor: He was like a child. He was so thrilled when he'd sing for me. I would tell him, 'Rafi saab, I am going to do this and I'm going to do that. I'm going to jump here and I'm going to leap there.' He used to react like a baby, full of shock and surprise on his face. He'd say, 'My God, you're really going to do that?' I'd say, 'Yes. That's why you'd better sing like that.' And he'd be pleasantly surprised when I showed him the results on the screen. I remember the song, '*Taareef karoun kya uski*' in *Kashmir in Kali.* I asked the music director, O.P. Nayyar, to end the song by repeating the catch line many times. And I asked Rafi saab to build each repetition with more force, more power, more pitch – and he did it! When they all saw the song on the screen, everyone leapt to their feet. Rafi saab rang me up and so did

Asha Bhosle. She rang me in the middle of the night and said she loved it.

Asha Bhosle, like her elder sister, Lata Mangeshkar, started her career as a child actress. In fact, the Mangeshkar sisters appeared together in the 1945 film *Badi Maa*. Like Lata, young Asha was also trained by their father, classical singer Dinanath Mangeshkar. But it took her many more years to become a leading playback singer, and it was only in the late 1950s, when she was closely associated with music director O.P. Nayyar, that Asha Bhosle really made it. At one stage in her career, S.D. Burman took her under his wing and encouraged her to follow Geeta Dutt's erotically suggestive singing style. Asha Bhosle's '*Aaiye meherban*' in *Howrah Bridge* (1958, Shakti Samanta; composer O.P. Nayyar) showed that she was in a class of her own when it came to seductive singing. No wonder, then, that she ended up singing all the best songs for vamp goddesses like Helen, and for screen characters who were more liberal and less perfect than the heroines.

Asha Bhosle's second marriage was to composer R.D. Burman, and together they modernized film music. Burman's compositions were fresh and funky, and the numbers he composed for his wife remain big favourites with young audiences. Asha Bhosle's fame and talent have inspired many Asian bands in Britain including Cornershop, whose hit song 'Brimful of Asha' is a tribute to this extraordinary singer.

Helen: Asha Bhosle sang the songs for me. The one I liked was 'Monica, my darling' from *Caravan*. During the recording of the song, Ashaji would ask who would be performing it on screen and if they told her it was me doing it, she would give that extra, you know, go, in it.

Among the current generation of female playback singers, the hugely talented Kavita Krishnamurthy and the excellent Alka Yagnik have a large following, singing for the new screen heroines such as Aishwarya Rai, Kajol, Karishma Kapoor and Rani Mukerji. The turning point in Kavita Krishnamurthy's career came with her rendition of 'Hawa Hawaii' from Mr India (1981, Shekhar Kapur; composers Laxmikant-Pyarelal), picturized on the brilliant Sridevi. Kavita Krishnamurthy has now been singing for the cinema for over fifteen years, during which time she has sung more than 1,000 songs. She prefers to sing for actresses whose speaking voices match her own. This gentle and gifted singer explains how the process of playback works today:

Kavita Krishnamurthy: The phone rings – it's usually the music director who calls, not the producer. He says, 'Madam, are you free in two days from now at three o'clock? We have a song for you.' I find rehearsals are not required in ninety-nine per cent of the songs that I have been singing in recent times. So I get to the recording studio and there I hear the tune for the first time. If the song is very difficult, they send me a cassette of the tune beforehand. Otherwise, I get to the studio, the lyricist tells me the words of the song and I write them down. The music director then explains what the song and the movie are all about and who the heroine is – that's if they know themselves. The music director plays the tune on the harmonium and teaches me the song.

Then the recordist plays the track once or twice for me to mark my cues – where I come in and where I'm out. It's nice if the song is a duet because the male playback singer and I get to sing together and emote together. But nowadays, people are so busy that the male singer isn't usually around and I have to record my part separately. The song is then recorded in an hour or maximum two hours.

In the old days, we used to record a song with all the musicians there. And God forbid if I made a mistake – the poor guys would have to start all over again. Sometimes a song would take fifty takes and five hours. But I remember the song 'Hawa Hawaii' was recorded in one take. When I'm ready to sing, that's when I think the switch goes on. Your body leaves the studio and you are in Switzerland or Kashmir or one of those lovely places. I am wearing beautiful clothes, there's natural beauty all around me. I think of a young girl who is eighteen and how she would go about singing the song. So it's basically imagination.

With the exception of Lata Mangeshkar and Asha Bhosle, the established playback singers of Hindi film music have passed away. There are many talented singers singing today for the new stars, but it seems unlikely that they will have anything like the impact of their predecessors. Music director Laxmikant, whose work with Pyarelal straddled forty years of film music, remained a key music director up to his death in 1998. Laxmikant will never forget the impact of the great names in playback singing:

Laxmikant: Rafi saab sang so many songs for us. He is the soul in 'Chahounga Main Tujhe'. The last song he ever recorded was for one of our tunes that featured in the 1980 film Aas Paas. The last song that Mukeshji ever recorded was one of ours – that song was 'Chanchal Sheetal' for Raj Kapoor's film Satyam Shivam Sundaram in 1978. I believe there will be good playback singers in the future. But singers like Mohammed Rafi, Kishore Kumar, Mukeshji, Lataji and Asha – to talk about them is like showing the sun a mirror.

Besides the many important singers, many great lyricists have worked in cinema, including Shams Lucknavi, Safdar Aah, Nakshab, Pradeep, D.N. Madhok, Qamar Jalalabadi, Pandit Narendra Sharma, Kidar Sharma and P.L. Santoshi. But the songwriters who have had the greatest influence on film music include Sahir Ludhianvi, Shailendra, Shakeel Badayuni, Majrooh Sultanpuri, Raja Mehdi, Ali Khan, Rajinder Krishen, Kaifi Azmi, Hasrat Jaipuri and Anand Bakshi. Although many gifted lyricists were more famous as songwriters, their individual work as poets had been established in the Urdu literary world before they entered the world of cinema. In his excellent essay 'Urdu, Awadh and the Tawaif', author Mukul Kesavan points out how Urdu influenced both the language and the lyrics of Hindi cinema: 'It is ironic but true that Hindi cinema is the last strong-hold of Urdu in independent India, its last haven in a sea of language bigotry. It is appropriate that this be so because the Hindi film has been fashioned out of the rhetorical and demotic resources of Urdu.' (Forging Identities, Gender, Communities *and the State*, ed. Zoya Hasan, Kali for Women, Delhi. 1994)

Many of the early film lyricists lived traumatic lives. Shailendra was alleged to have committed suicide in 1966 and Sahir Ludhianvi, who died in 1980, famously remained unfulfilled in his love life. These extraordinary songwriters contributed vastly to lifting the overall impact of unremarkable and repetitive screenplays by giving such films a literary flavour. Their songs are characterized by reflections on society and culture, often including outrage at social inequities, injustices and inhumanity, but their genius is equally adept at expressing intense emotions and private feelings. Sahir's Marxist philosophy and somewhat failing belief in Nehru's vision for a new India were expressed in songs such as '*Chino-o-Arab Hamara, Rehne Ko Ghar Nahin Hai, Hindustan Hamara*' ('China and Arabia are ours, we have no roof over our heads but India belongs to us') – from the 1958 film *Phir Subah Hogi* – and *Pyaasa*'s '*Jinhain Naaz Hai Hind Par Vo Kahaan Hai*' ('Where are those who claim to be proud of India?'). He was equally at ease when it came to expressing delicate emotions in the love songs and the *qawwalis* of P.L. Santoshi's *Barsaat ki Raat* (1960; composer Roshan). Sahir maintained that Indian films were too concerned with 'how to say' a thing, paying little attention to 'what to say'. In an interview in 1962, he outlined his intentions for his songs: 'It has always been my endeavour, as far as possible, to bring film songs closer to creative poetry and to convey through them, to the people, social and political principles.' Sahir, who was actively involved in the anti-British movement, was a known leftist. Born in 1921 in Ludhiana, Punjab, as Abdul Hayee (he later took on the pen name Sahir, which means magician), as a bachelor Sahir's name was linked romantically to the poetess Amrita

Pritam and later to the singer Sudha Malhotra. Composer S.D. Burman and producer/director Chetan Anand were instrumental in helping him during the early part of his career, a debt that Sahir repeatedly acknowledged throughout his life. Through the 1960s, he wrote fabulous songs for films such as *Hum Dono* (1961), *Gumrah* (1963), *Taj Mahal* (1963) and *Waqt* (1965). Though Sahir did not write for many films in the 1970s, the title song from the film *Kabhi Kabhie* (1976) alone is proof of his extraordinary talent.

Javed Akhtar: You will find the most beautiful songs in the 1950s and 1960s. The first lyricist who comes to mind is Sahir Ludhianvi. You know, usually film songs are written on a given tune, and obviously if the tune is already composed and the words have to fit, the tune takes on more importance. Despite this, Sahir Saab has written wonderful songs and even if the words are not sung, the lyrics themselves have beauty and magic. I am thinking of the S.D. Burman song from *Jaal*, 'Yeh Raat Ye Chandni Phir Kahaan'.

Like Sahir Ludhianvi, the great lyricist Shailendra also stayed at the top of his profession for over two decades. His amazing songs, which mixed Hindi and Urdu, were marked by their simplicity of expression and delicacy of language. Shailendra worked for the Indian Railways and was a member of the left-wing Indian People's Theatre Association; it was only the need to provide for his family that led Shailendra to Raj Kapoor. He wrote two songs for Kapoor's *Barsaat* (the title song and 'Patli Qamar Hai'), and was paid 500 rupees for the work. Insecure about a future in films, however, Shailendra did not leave his day job until five years after *Barsaat,* and even when he was writing *'Awaara Hun'* he was still working for the Indian Railways. His mix of wisdom in songs such as *'Wahan Kaun Hai Tera Musafir'* ('O traveller, who awaits you?') from *Guide* recalled the writings of great folk poets. Shailendra's Marxism and deep compassion came out in his songs, which always reached out to both ordinary people and to the literary-minded.

Kaifi Azmi was another important Urdu poet and lyricist. Kaifi Azmi was born into a *zamindari* (land-owning) family in Mizan, a village near Azamgarh, Uttar Pradesh. His family were not rich but were talented in the arts. Kaifi Azmi began writing poetry at eleven. His father originally wanted him to be a *maulvi* (Muslim priest), but in 1945, just nineteen years old, he moved to Bombay and joined the Communist Party. In 1947, he married a young Hyderabadi woman, Shaukat, much against her family's wishes. Shaukat Azmi later became a well-known stage actress at the Indian People's Theatre Association, and their daughter is the celebrated star, Shabana Azmi. Kaifi Azmi's life was dominated by his commitment to the Communist Party and in order to make ends meet, he turned to cinema. Although Azmi didn't write many songs compared to his contemporaries, his lyrics for films such as *Kaagaz Ke Phool* and *Haqeeqat* are unforgettable.

The fiery Urdu poet and songwriter Majrooh Sultanpuri rose to fame in 1949 writing for *Andaaz.* During five decades of creating film music, Majrooh Sultanpuri worked with the widest range of music composers and directors. He wrote beautiful love songs including *'Chand Phir Nikala',* fun songs such as *'Jaane Kahan Gaya Jigar Mera Ji',* rock 'n' roll numbers like *'Aja Aja Main Hun Pyar Tera'* and *'Chura Liya Hai Tune Jo Dil Ko'* (famously remixed in the 1990s by Bally Sagoo) and a recent hit by A.R. Rahman, 'Kismet Se Tum Hum Ko Mile'. Unlike most lyricists, who prefer to write their lines first and then have them set to music, Majrooh gained a reputation for writing effortlessly to a tune. In a conversation with Sheila Vesuna in India's The Sunday Observer in 1994, he commented, 'Of course, it is better if the words are written first. But this has been one of my abilities. Would you say that 'Ye Hai Reshmi Zulfon Ka Andhera' was written after the tune was composed? But that is a fact.' Majrooh Sultanpuri's death in 2000 marked the end of an era of songwriters whose excellence is unlikely to be matched.

Music is still of primary importance in cinema today. But society's values and notions of romance have changed, and it would be inappropriate for songs now to reflect the same intensity of sentiment and feeling, or convey the sense of social protest, that informed earlier melodies. Songs are now more prosaic and words carry less weight. But even though the balance is tipped in favour of dance numbers, contemporary lyricists – including Gulzar, Sameer, Mehboob and Javed Akhtar – still try to introduce poetry into their work. The songs of Gulzar and Javed Akhtar create mood and atmosphere using a higher Urdu vocabulary. Javed Akhtar explains how he goes about writing a song:

> **Javed Akhtar:** The music director gives us a tune, the director gives us a situation in which the song will take place, and then we write the words for the tune. I write songs for Hindi movies – maybe I should call them Hindi-Urdu movies. I would rather not tell you how easily most of the songs come to me, because my

producers will start paying me less! But there are certain songs that do not need any cleverness. Such songs need tremendous simplicity and a surrender of ego; they should be so gentle, and so soft and have an ethereal quality. That kind of song takes time because it's always an effort to shed cleverness and smartness and find innocence within yourself. Hindi pictures are basically meant to appeal to the emotions, to feelings, so it is quite logical that they will have poetry, and poetry in the form of songs.

Songs continue to extend the life of thousands of movies, defining the meaning of love, describing the many shades of emotion, eulogizing the beauty of the beloved, conveying the pain of separation, conversing and coercing through poetry and glorifying the splendour of nature. Along the way, film music has also played its part in defining the essence of the Indian character. Special mention must be made here of the central role played by All India Radio, particularly the station Vividh Bharati, in making film music part of the fabric of Indian life. (In cinema's early days, the Indian government did not want to promote film music, but finally All India Radio had to bow down to popular pressure.) *Farmaish* (requests) radio programmes were key in connecting listeners to both the radio and to film music. Famously, the highest number of requests for favourite songs that the station received came from Jhumritaliya (an obscure Bihar town). So numerous were the requests that considerable speculation arose as to whether such a place really existed. In fact, these requests came from clients who frequented a tea-shop and would come in at a fixed hour to listen to the radio.

While having tea, they were able to look forward to the radio presenter mentioning their names along with their request for a top song. The rise of film music was further helped by the early years of commercial broadcasting, in particular by Radio Ceylon. The radio show 'Binaca Hit Parade', hosted by Ameen Sayani, had a following of millions across the Indian subcontinent and was instrumental in popularizing not only the film songs themselves, but also in making music directors and playback singers household names. Sayani would make it a point of informing his listeners, for example, that their favourite song, *Duniya Ke Rakhwale* from the film *Baiju Bawra*, was composed by Naushad, with lyrics written by Shakeel Badayuni and sung by Mohammed Rafi, giving everyone their due. The coming of the affordable transistor radio in the 1960s helped to spread film music to every corner of the subcontinent. Moreover, rather than decreasing the popularity of film songs, the introduction of television and satellite channels has doubled and tripled their following.

It would not be an exaggeration to say that Hindi film music has now become one of the most important and all-pervasive elements of Indian culture. Film songs can be heard virtually everywhere in India, and the folk music that originally inspired it is now less popular than its cinematic version. Wedding bands that once played traditional wedding songs now play the latest hit numbers instead. Since the early 1990s, Hindi film music has also entered the club scene. In a cover story for an edition of Indian magazine *Sunday* from early 1995, journalists Priya Sahgal and Vasundha Gore noted, 'Suddenly, India's elite has discovered its own music – via the West. For all of the last two months, the number one song at every discotheque has been

"*Chura Liya*", originally featured in the 1973 Zeenat Aman movie *Yaadon Ki Baraat*. "*Chura Liya*" is the work of Bally Sagoo, alias Baljeet Singh Sagoo, born in New Delhi but newly reimported to India via Birmingham.' ('Dance to the Music', *Sunday*, 15-21 January 1995)

The trend of DJs playing film music in clubs started in India with Amitabh Bachchan's raunchy '*Jumma, Chumma De De*' from *Hum* (1991, Mukul Anand; composers Laxmikant-Pyarelal), based on the music by West African singer Mory Kante. '*Jumma, Chumma De De*' ('Jumma, give us a kiss') became a smash hit at discos and played at 'the best parties, and the best slums' ('Dance to the Music', *Sunday*). A whole host of Hindi film tunes were subsequently remixed in hip-hop, rap and jungle styles by many Asian bands in India and in Britain, giving rise to a pop alternative to film music. The popularity of music channels such as Channel V and MTV Asia has provided a platform for a new music scene. However, the most watched shows on Channel V, such as *Mangta Hai*, *Videocon Flashback* and *The Great Indian Manovigyanik Show*, still rely on film clips from old and new Hindi movies. Jaaved Jaaferi (son of the comedian Jagdeep) is an actor and dancer who became a huge television personality as a presenter of TV music shows. He explains why Hindi film songs have the special power they do:

Jaaved Jaaferi: Regional accents and languages are different from state to state. You watch a film and don't understand Hindi, you don't understand, the rites and rituals in this particular wedding ceremony because you come from a different tradition, demographically different. But the music, that's fine. That's why we have songs and dances. The songs are so important in Hindi films. A lot of time and money is spent on the song picturizations to make them look good. You may have a hundred dancers, and every third line of the song, there's a different costume change and a different location. Now Switzerland has become the 'in' thing, Europe has become the 'in' thing, and suddenly in the middle of the Dharavi slums, you cut to Switzerland – it's a dream sequence. And the hero is singing a song and dancing.

Chapter Eight

DANCING
TO THE MUSIC

To fully examine the extraordinary output of the vast number of music directors who have shaped Hindi cinema is the work of a dozen books. Hindi films are often subject to much criticism and disdain, but music directors usually escape the flak, attracting floods of praise from critics and audiences alike. By the 1950s, they were regarded as being as important as the film's director, their names appearing equal in size on film posters and publicity material.

Though the individual contributions of many lyricists cannot be underestimated, their songs have usually won greater fame when they have opted to work in tandem with a music director. Sahir Ludhianvi is best remembered for his work with S.D. Burman; Shakeel Badayuni and Naushad were a celebrated team; Shailendra and Hasrat Jaipuri were famously linked with music directors Shankar-Jaikishan and Anand Bakshi with Laxmikant-Pyarelal. As the last two examples listed here indicate, many music directors have worked in a close-knit team; their names consequently became compounded together, as in Husnlal-Bhagatram, Kalyanji-Anandji, Raam-Laxman, Nadeem-Shravan, Shiv-Hari, Anand-Milund, and Jatin-Lalit.

Inspired and guided by composers such as Khemchand Prakash, Anil Biswas and Timir Baran, the leading music directors of the 1940s and 1950s brought their musical folk origins to their compositions. Ghulam Haider set a trend with *Khazanchi* in 1941, in which he brought the folk music of Punjab to the fore, as well as prioritizing certain percussion instruments, such as the *dholak*. S.D. Burman, Hemant Kumar and Salil Choudhury became renowned for introducing music from their native Bengal. Naushad Ali's compositions showed the influence of the folk tradition of Uttar Pradesh, and C. Ramchandra's melodies can be traced to Marathi folk music. In his excellent book *Cassette Culture*, Peter Manuel notes that, 'Film music, like Indian cinema in general, can be seen to reflect in its own way the dialectic interaction of tradition and modernity, city and countryside and national identity and the West. Most film songs combine Western and indigenous elements. Imported instruments like congas, synthesizers, horns and especially violins are used alongside tabla and dholak drums and melodic instruments like sitar and sarod.' (*Cassette Culture*, University of Chicago Press, 1993)

P.K. Nair: A real change in the classical tradition came in the 1940s with music director Ghulam Haider from Lahore. Then there was the producer Dalsukh M.

Pancholi, who brought in Punjabi folk music. It is said that the *dholak* replaced the harmonium, which was the main instrument used until that time. In the 1940s, the other music directors who came into prominence were Naushad, a disciple of Khemchand Prakash, Ghulam Mohammed and many others. C. Ramachandra brought in a new style of his own and was also a singer. C. Ramachandra had acted in a couple of films too. He integrated Western music, the rumba, the samba, Mexican and south Asian music. Then we had S.D. Burman, who brought in the Bengali tradition associated with Rabindra Sangeet and there was the excellent Madan Mohan and Roshan. The 1950s was a period when the music director had much say. In fact, music directors were more appreciated and respected than perhaps film directors. In terms of market value, sometimes the music directors were even paid more than the directors. So that shows how important music had become in the development of Indian films. It was only in the mid-seventies and eighties that music took a back seat in cinema.

The best music can be dated to the 1950s and early 1960s – the black and white era. In the 1960s, colour photography became widespread and with it a tendency arose to indulge anything colourful. Social issues that featured in the films of the 1950s lost out to lighter romantic themes. The ultimate appeal of these films lay in the number of love songs, set in heavenly locations, that they offered. Beautiful mountains, cascading waters and serene lakesides bordered by garish flower beds formed the backdrop to the dancing heroine, who appeared in a new outfit for every different musical refrain.

The cinema of the 1970s and 1980s, characterized among other things by an increase in screen violence, marked a decline in quality music; violent action films were hardly an appropriate place for romantic songs. Many established music directors died during this decade, and the new generation of music directors struggled to make any impact. By the end of the 1980s, however, cinema trends were changing once again, through the revival of the ever-popular teenage love stories. The success of films such as Mansoor Khan's 1988 hit *Qayamat Se Qayamat Tak* (composers Anand-Milund) and *Maine Pyar Kiya* (composers Raam-Laxman) from the following year announced the return of music as a vital component of Indian cinema.

Anu Malik has been writing film music for many years (his father, Sardar Malik, was also a music director) but he received his major break with the 1993 film *Baazigar*. He believes, 'No music, no Hindi cinema.'

Anu Malik: I've written music for about 300 films. I started work at sixteen; I've been in the business for almost twenty-one years. It's no mean achievement to be where I am, because you've got to really work hard. Hindi films require music all the time. In fact, the Hindi film industry depends on music. What happens is that people listen to the audio track, either on cassettes or on the radio, or they see the song clip on television. They hear the music of a particular film with say, Salman Khan, Hritik Roshan or Abhishek Bachchan. After they hear the music, they form an opinion about the film; if they like the music, the film is assured of a very good opening, and if, God forbid, they don't like the music, well, all hell breaks loose, because the financiers, the producers and the distributors are worried, and the stars are worried, because there is a possibility the film may not open well. You see, distributors release over 200 prints and they want to see that the crowd comes into the theatre on the very first day. If the first week has a 100 per cent collection, there is a possibility the film will go into the second week. Music makes the world go round, at least in India.

The most brilliant music director to emerge in the 1990s is A.R. Rahman, and his compositions for Mani Ratnam's excellent films, *Roja*, *Bombay* and *Dil Se*, brought him to the attention of the Hindi film industry. Mani Ratnam sees Rahman as someone who is prepared to break conventions in terms of music. Such risk-taking has paid off: today, producers form queues in Rahman's Madras home, hoping that he will agree to compose music for their next production. Despite his success, Rahman is deeply modest, a shy thirty-three-year-old who is a devout Muslim, praying five times a day. He is also a brilliant singer and his international concerts, so far aimed exclusively at the Asian community, are sell-outs. Rahman is currently composing music for Andrew Lloyd Webber's new musical, to be launched in 2002.

A.R. Rahman prefers working through the night; his compositions are characterized by his thoughtful combination of contemporary sounds with more traditional Eastern rhythms and melodies. He uses a variety of playback singers together with an intriguing mix of instrumentation. However,

Rahman's humility and piety are more important to him than his success:

> **A.R. Rahman**: The essence of Sufism is about love. Music and Sufism go very well together. Somehow it inspires you to think in a divine way rather than just think I'll do this song. For me, the next stage of everything is completely unknown. I am almost like a boat on a river without a sail and I keep going. I'm surprised when good things happen and I'm cool when something bad happens. I trust God and it helps me to get rid of unnecessary things like jealousy, and greed and all this stuff. I'm not fully out of it. But I am trying. It makes me like oil on water, I'm there and not there and I'm not sticking to anything.

Song and dance are the most original aspects of Indian cinema and Rahman's music marks him out as unique. His work in *Rangeela* (1995), *Pukar* (1999), *Taal* (1999) and *Zubeida* (2001) has resulted in the most exciting film soundtracks in recent years. Like R.D. Burman before him, Rahman is in the process of creating a new era in Indian film music. His music not only brings alive a film's soundtrack, but also inspires choreographers to create the most exciting dance numbers that are challenging for the stars and among the most entertaining scenes for the audience.

Like singing, dancing talent has been an essential requirement for aspiring stars for almost as long as the Indian film industry has existed. In the early days, classical and semi-classical dances were featured, and certain genres like the historical and the costume drama boasted lavish dance numbers involving seductive court dancers and big sets, like S.S. Vasan's *Chandralekha* (1948), that has the most spectacular screen dance. And if a hero such as Ashok Kumar in the 1943 film *Kismet* could not dance, then the talented Mumtaz Ali (comedian Mehmood's father) would perform a traditional routine that would become one of the movie's high points. *Kalpana* (1948) was the most unusual dance film of Indian cinema, and was made by Uday Shankar, the internationally celebrated dancer and choreographer. Shankar built his narrative around extraordinary set pieces that were both innovative and original. At one point it seemed as though *Kalpana* would start a new film genre in Hindi cinema, one that relied solely on dance, although this proved not to be the case. But dancers who had worked with Uday Shankar, such as Zohra Sehgal (also a reputed actress) and the French-born Madame Simkie, and director/actor Guru Dutt, certainly had a major influence on film choreography. Madame Simkie's most famous work is the dream sequence in *Awaara*, which clearly shows Shankar's influence. In 2001, the celebrated painter M.F. Hussain paid tribute to Uday Shankar's style in his own unusual dance film, *Gaja Gamini*, featuring the actress/dancer Madhuri Dixit.

Over the years, Hindi cinema has evolved a distinct genre of dance, the 'filmi dance', a hybrid of all forms imaginable that includes great emphasis on pelvic movement, familiarly known as '*jhatkas* and *matkas*'. In south India, the film dance is called the 'cinematic dance'. In film jargon, choreographers are known as 'dance directors' and 'dance masters'. Although many actresses, particularly from the south – including Padmini, Vyjayantimala, Waheeda Rahman, Hema Malini, Rekha and

Sridevi – were trained in dance, they usually relied on the dance director to choreograph the song. The most renowned early choreographers included Azurie, Krishna Kumar, Sitara Devi, Gopi Krishna, Hiralal (who choreographed the famous dances in *Guide*) and Sohanlal (celebrated for his choreography in *Sahib Bibi aur Ghulam* [1962, Abrar Alvi] and *Jewel Thief* [1967, Vijay Anand]), Sathyanarayan, Satyakumar and Sachin Shankar, who between them created some truly sublime moments in dance.

These dance masters were followed by a new generation from the 1970s on, including Master Kamal, who was at one point, Amitabh Bachchan's favourite dance director, and Vijay-Oscar, who introduced disco numbers, breakdance and jazz in the 1980s films *Qurbani* (1980, Feroz Khan) with Zeenat Aman, *Karz* (1980, Subhash Ghai) with Rishi Kapoor, *Disco Dancer* (1982, B. Subhash) with Mithun Chakravorty and *Dance Dance* (1987, B. Subhash). Chinni and Rekha Prakash's choreography for the Bachchan number '*Jumma, Chumma De De*' gave dancing an unprecedented importance in the 1990s. Indeed, so vital did dance become that choreographers became the real stars of the film. They were responsible for directing the musical scenes in tandem with the film director and today they continue to provide Hindi movies with their 'repeat value' – the audience comes back to see a dance number again and again and may happily walk out as soon as the scene is over.

To its credit, the Indian film industry, which is largely male-dominated, has encouraged women choreographers, of whom the biggest names in recent years are Saroj Khan and Farah Khan. Since the 1980s, Saroj Khan has proved herself to be the choreographer with the greatest influence on the heroine's dance. She is a strong, emotional woman whose passion has always been dancing. One of her favourite dance sequences is the amazing 'Aplam Chaplam' from Azaad (1955, S.M.S. Naidu, composer C. Ramachandran) performed by Sai and Subbalaxmi, whose looks and skill make this sequence one of the most charming of the black and white era. Saroj Khan recounts how, as a child, she would lock herself up in a room and dance for hours. Her mother believed Saroj to be unwell and took her to a doctor. The doctor recognized young Saroj's talent, however, and introduced her to the world of films through a friend.

Early in her career, Saroj Khan worked as assistant to Sohanlal. When Sohanlal left with Raj Kapoor for Europe to shoot Sangam, the fourteen-year-old Saroj was asked by the disgruntled producer to compose the qawwali number for actress Nutan in his film Dil Hi to Hai (1963, P.L. Santoshi and C.L. Rawal, composer Roshan). Her first song was the delicate and sublle 'Nighahen Milane Ko Jee Chhahata Hai', which turned out to be the highlight of the movie (Saroj Khan herself appears in the front line of dancers in this lovely song). Despite such a promising start, for many years to come she chose not to work in films, opting instead to live in Dubai, looking after her husband and children. When Saroj Khan returned to Bombay in the 1980s, Subhash Ghai asked her to choreograph his films Vidhata (1982), Hero (1983) and Ram Lakhan (1989).

By the end of the eighties, Saroj Khan had succeeded in changing the audience's perception of Sridevi and Madhuri Dixit by turning them into sexy dance Goddesses in films such as Mr India (1987, Shekhar Kapur) and Tezaab (1988, N. Chandra). Saroj Khan's choreography nearly always defies current trends – if songs in a particular decade are sedate and slow, she introduces pace and movement; if songs are Westernized, she brings back Indian dance steps. Most importantly, she understands how to use close-ups and wide shots to maximum effect. She knows how to get Aishwarya Rai flying in the energetic number 'Nimbooda Nimbooda' from *Hum Dil De Chuke Sanam* (1999) and make Madhuri Dixit move erotically in 'Dhak Dhak Karne Laga', from 1992's *Beta*. With their hair blowing in the breeze (evoking the song scenes from the black and white era, in which the beautiful heroine was nearly always back-lit, with a breeze gently blowing across her), and suggestive dance steps, Saroj Khan's heroines seduce audiences like those of no other choreographer. She understands how important dance has always been to Indian culture:

Saroj Khan: We dance at any pretext. We dance at weddings, we dance at Diwali and at Holi. All emotional expressions are shown in songs. If songs and dances were missing from our movies, I doubt if the audience would enter a cinema hall. In the past few years, there's been too much western influence, too much MTV. Every song has twenty dancers moving in breakdance style. The same look, the same dance. So I have been composing Indian-style dancing in the recent films. My dance steps must be enticing, so the audience will watch. A young child or a young woman should be able to copy the dance steps. If we were to use a pure classical form, no one would watch any more. We have to be full of spice! *[Smiles]*

Farah Khan has worked with all the top names of Hindi film, and her choreography has helped make actors and actresses into stars. She is particularly gifted at composing modern dance routines for male actors. A stunning example of her skill occurs in Mani Ratnam's *Dil Se* (composer A.R. Rahman) of 1998, in which we see the hero, Shahrukh Khan, and some thirty dancers perform a rhythmic dance to the song 'Chaiyya Chaiyya' on an open carriage of a moving train. It is rumoured that it was this particular dance that prompted Andrew Lloyd Webber to ask music director A.R. Rahman to compose for him. Farah Khan explains what Hindi film dancing is all about:

Farah Khan: Hindi films have a lot of dance genres. There's Indian classical dancing, western dancing, ballet, rock 'n' roll, flamenco, modern dancing – everything; what we call a typical 'filmi' dance, which is just a mix of everything. I have been a choreographer and dance director for the last six years and I've done about thirty films. I take the song and choreograph it first with my dancers and then I work with the main hero and heroine. Every Hindi film has to have six or seven dances, and that's the big moment the audience waits for.

Although most actors depend on choreographers to help them along, there have also been a number of 'star-dancers', whose dancing skills complemented their acting. Master Bhagwan was perhaps the earliest of such artistes. His reign did not outlive the 1950s, but he changed the way heroes (including Amitabh Bachchan) danced for years afterwards. Bhagwan's Latin American steps in 1951's *Albela* (which he also directed) were particularly influential on subsequent performers. In later years, famous star-dancers have included Shammi Kapoor (who did his own dances), Mithun Chakravorty (famous for his disco dancing in bizarre costumes under psychedelic lighting), Govinda, Kamal Haasan and Tamil superstar Prabhu Deva (heavily influenced by Michael Jackson). The popularity of all these male stars, including current A-list actors like Shahrukh Khan, Aamir Khan, Salman Khan and Hritik Roshan, is considerably enhanced by their ability to move well on the dancefloor.

Among the first of the female star-dancers was the delicate Cuckoo, who started her career in the late 1940s. Cuckoo's skills were limited, but the freedom and abandon with which she could dance made her greatly appealing when juxtaposed against the inhibited heroine. Cuckoo introduced the young Helen, who was soon labelled 'the queen of the dancing girls'. Helen could dance in any style with apparently little effort, whether jiving in a cabaret number, moving to the beat in a huge champagne glass or hopping in rhythm from key to key on a gigantic typewriter. Every element of the cinema audience loved Helen, from the lower stalls to the dress circle. She had character and sexuality and was never considered vulgar, even though she played the vamp countless times.

Other female star-dancers included Minoo Mumtaz (comedian Mehmood's sister), Kumkum, Madhumati (who somewhat resembled Helen, which wasn't an advantage), Fariyal, Mumtaz (who, like Jayshree and Sandhya before her, became a big star), Kalpana Iyer and Aruna Irani (regarded as a lead actress-cum-dancer in the 1970s). Padma Khanna, a favoured protégée of the celebrated dance director Gopi Krishna (who choreographed the splendid dances in *Mughal-e-Azam* [1960, K. Asif]), became an overnight star following her cabaret number in *Johnny Mera Naam* (1970, Vijay Anand), although she was not to have a long screen career. Contemporary female stars are nearly all terrific dancers, from Sridevi to Karishma Kapoor.

Sanjay Leela Bhansali is one of the few directors today who has had formal training in dance. His early work in films involved directing the songs in Vidhu Vinod Chopra's *Parinda* (1989) and *1942, A Love Story* (1994) before he made his own first feature in 1996, *Khamoshi*.

Sanjay Leela Bhansali: As a child, I had no other passion in life but to listen to film songs on the radio. I would visualize how I would dance on this tune, or how I would shoot that song. And then I learnt classical dancing, Odissi, for three and a half years. I also studied editing at the Film and Television Institute in Pune. Editing means the use of rhythm, the sound, the relationship with emotions that equally flow through a certain raga. My passion was not to go and see a movie; my passion was to see how Helen danced in a film. How did they shoot Vyjayantimala or Waheeda Rahman as they danced?

I was fascinated with *Guide*; I saw it again and again because of Waheedaji's snake dance. Here's a character, a dancer who has been repressed by her husband, and has not danced for years, and she suddenly breaks into a dance. At the end, she's exhausted and falls down. I thought that was the most memorable dance sequence in Hindi films. Vijay Anand for me is the best director of songs and dances. His shot breakdown is extremely beautiful; even today I still cannot understand how he moves the camera and the actors – even in simple love duets. He picturized big dance numbers beautifully, like the *Jewel Thief* song '*Honton Pe Aisi Baat*' by S.D. Burman.

In contrast to the static songs of the early sound films, the pace of today's songs is fast and furious. Filmmakers recognize a number of schools of song picturizations, including those of Bimal Roy, Raj Kapoor and Guru Dutt. An excellent example of song picturization – indeed, one that elevates it to an art form – is provided by Raj Kapoor's black and white *Awaara*, the film that started the popular trend of setting songs within a dream. *Awaara*'s majestic three-level set matches a three-part song that reveals the three emotional states of its hero and heroine, choreographed by Madame Simkie. The first state is the pain of separation, followed by the pleasure and joy of union and, finally, punishment that is inescapable. The first part of this nine-minute sequence shows the heroine Rita (Nargis) in a celestial and idyllic abode calling out in song to Raj ('*Tere Bina Aag Yeh Chandni, Tu Aa Ja*' – 'The moonlight is fire without you, come to me'). At the end of this first song, the camera descends into a hellish hole where the hero Raj, surrounded by evil spirits and demons, cries in anguish, '*Yeh nahin zindagi zindagi ye nahin*' ('Not a life like this, no'). Raj somehow manages to climb out of this inferno – a metaphor for his feelings of being trapped in a life of crime – and finds himself in Rita's celestial abode, a place of redemption. Here, the song becomes a prayer evoking the name of Lord Shiva. Rita rushes to guide Raj up the grand stairway and so enter a new phase of his life. This part of the dream has the third and wonderful Lata Mangeshkar song, '*Ghar Aya Mera Pardesi*' ('My beloved has come home at last'). The last phase of the dream, so full of metaphor, symbols and psychological meaning, depicts Raj and Rita climbing a winding tower leading higher and higher into the sky. Here, instead of union with God, the devil (in the form of the bandit Jagga) awaits Raj, who desperately calls out to Rita to save him. But his cries are in vain. Reality becomes disjointed and fragmented and, like the façade of Raj's life, this new-found paradise crumbles; the dream becomes a nightmare. Raj wakes up, jumps out of his bed, frightened and shaken, and rushes to his mother who is in the adjoining room, saying, 'Ma, I want to be good. I'll go hungry but I won't steal. People will respect me.'

Established occasions for songs, like the dream sequence, have long been a part of Indian films. These include the *mujra* (the golden-hearted prostitute dancing in a Kathak style in a brothel) and the Holi festival. These stock situations have never lost their appeal. But it's the 'wet sari' dance that has become an indispensable set piece in Indian films. Dance director Lollipop, known for choreographing the song, *'Aati Kya Khandala'*, performed by Aamir Khan and Rani Mukerji (*Ghulam*, 1999), notes that the 'wet sari' number must not only have the heroine wearing a sari, but also show the hero wearing a cap so we see drops of rain fall in front of his eyes. Lollipop observes, 'When the audience see this number, they think, ah, this is our song!' Psychotherapist Udayan Patel has his own take on this popular dance routine:

Udayan Patel: The gyrations are repeated and the use of the eyes, the use of the lips, all suggest overt sexuality. In our culture, we are split between living through private imaginations and social behaviour. In family entertainment, the family can hear and the family can see. So there is no kiss, there is no sex. If it's very explicit they can't ignore it. And parents will say this is not a good film, this is a bad film. I don't think producers want that divide because they will lose a big audience. So sexuality is expressed through dance and the movement of the body drenched by water – this type of dance has been there from the days of Raj Kapoor. Here you have dance movements that remind you of sexual intercourse without touching or kissing. The more vulgar movements create erotic fantasies, and the audience responds, and so you hear the cat calls. All heroines have a way of arousing in the audience active sexual fantasies and the more the fantasies, the greater the heroine's success.

The other popular cinematic song is the cross-dressing number, which originated in festivals such as Holi and still forms a part of wedding parties. This dance involves the hero dressing up as a woman and performing a raunchy song. Shahrukh Khan went one step further in *Duplicate* (1999): instead of dancing, he became involved in an elaborate action scene, dressed as a woman.

Shahrukh Khan: I will never do it again. I needed an operation because of that scene. They made me wear a corset with sticks in it that went into my abdomen and I got hurt. I mean, having a cleavage is difficult enough. Normally what happens is that when my co-star is getting ready, I'm like, 'Come on, *yaar*, hurry up!' And when I had to wear all that make-up, from eyelashes to the corset, the bra to the rouge and the wig. Now, I have an immense amount of respect for heroines. If a woman tells me 'Shahrukh, I'm going to take an hour and a half to get ready,' I say, 'Please, take two hours.' Hats off to all the actresses in the world if they have to do all this for one shot.

Recent directors such as Mani Ratnam, Sanjay Leela Bhansali, Dharmesh Darshan, Aditya Chopra and Karan Johar have shown themselves to be highly inventive in their song picturizations and prove that the best use of songs is when they reveal the inner emotions of characters and advance the narrative through poetry. Despite the fact that musical sequences in Hindi films were in many ways precursors of Western music videos, the roles have been reversed over time and now MTV culture dominates many typical song picturizations. Elaborate sets and travelogue locations provide the undeniable appeal of these big new numbers. But such lavish dance routines have a tendency to make Hindi film narrative more episodic, as they no longer work organically within the plot. Nor do the songs relate to the physicality and texture of Indian life. Lyricist Javed Akhtar admits, smiling, 'The song used to be like a scene in the film; now it has turned into some kind of mischievous child sitting on the shoulder of the script.'

Chapter Nine

THE ART OF ENTERTAINING MILLIONS

Indians genuinely love cinema. And no matter what the period of filmmaking, Indian directors are confident of a loyal following, but know they must keep audience taste and demands in mind. Deviating from expectations is something very few popular cinema directors dare – and this is true even in the area of casting. Filmmakers find that they are rarely successful if they cast an actor against the image he or she has secured as a star – if a hero is a hero, he cannot be seen to be weak and unable to flatten the villain. An audience for a film starring Dharmendra or Amitabh Bachchan expect to see a high body count. Stunt director Mahendra Varma remembers with great amusement an incident in the Punjab when Bengali director Hrishikesh Mukherjee, who is known for the more intelligent social film, cast Dharmendra and Amitabh Bachchan against type:

> **Mahendra Varma:** There were five Sikh friends in the Punjab who didn't read English, but they saw the poster of a film *Chupke Chupke* – the poster had a picture of Amitabh Bachchan and Dharmendra and that was enough, these five friends went in to see the film. But as you know, *Chupke Chupke* is a comedy. The audience came out disappointed and dejected. One of the friends complained that there wasn't a single fist fight, wrestling or jostling scene in this film. Another friend asked, 'What is the name of the film director?' The fellow who could read a little saw the poster and said, 'The director is someone called Rishki Pushki Mukherjee! [*laughs loudly*] This director has two lions in his movie and doesn't do anything with them.' Fighting is a must for audiences in the North and as Dharmendra and Amitabh Bachchan have the image of action heroes, how can the audience accept seeing them without action?

Binding actors to a set image goes beyond the action movie and extends to all other film genres. If actors are cast in one film as lovers, they cannot be cast in another as brother and sister, or mother and son. Perhaps the most famous example of this came with *Mother India*, in which Mehboob Khan resisted casting Dilip Kumar as Radha's son, Birju, because Nargis, who played Radha, had been seen in many movies as the object of Dilip Kumar's love. If the audience believes that an actor is having a love affair with an actress in real life and that alleged affair is reported widely in film magazines (of which there are many in India), then they will not accept them playing father and daughter. The director of *Khamoshi* has learned the hard way that taking risks in casting doesn't go down well with the paying punters:

Sanjay Leela Bhansali: I'll tell you what I went through in my first film, *Khamoshi*. The main character of the film is a deaf mute, who was played by Nana Patekar. Nana is known for his fiery dialogue delivery, and violent outbursts and speeches. And I cast him as a deaf man and so he cannot speak. First day, first show, I am in Liberty cinema. It hadn't been publicized that Nana Patekar was playing a deaf character – that was my big mistake. The trailers looked very promising and people rushed to the theatre. The film starts and Nana is seen communicating on screen through sign language. The audience in the lower stalls starts shouting, 'Nana! Talk! Please speak.' I just sank at Liberty Theatre, I just sank. I said, 'Gone, my film has gone.' They continued shouting, 'We want to hear you speak, *yaar*, come on, speak!' As if Nana could hear them, and Nana was going to start speaking. Then actress Seema Biswas appears. She plays Nana's screen wife and together they try to wake their newborn child through sign language. Nana brushes Seema aside in frustration because the child does not react, and he gets angry with Seema. The minute Nana hits her, the audience yells, 'Phoolan Devi!' Because Seema Biswas had played the role of Phoolan Devi, the bandit queen, they shouted, 'Phoolan Devi, shoot him! Shoot him!' I thought, 'Gone. My film is a disaster from the word go.' The whole audience is laughing and I'm sitting in Liberty crying. A few days later, a distributor from Delhi came to me saying, 'Sir, in Delhi they are hooting away. In the last scene, please make Nana speak.' I said, 'But he's deaf and in the last scene he's dying; if he were to speak, he would have spoken much earlier in the film, how can I make him speak at the end of the film?' The distributor touches my feet and says, 'Please, go to a recording studio and add Nana's dialogue. Your film will do great business.' I told him I cannot go against my convictions and make my character speak. But why did this distributor tell me this? Because the audience demands it.

As in the West, Indian audiences come to form close relationships with the stars that go way beyond the screen. Young men want to walk and talk like Amitabh Bachchan, or have a Shahrukh Khan or Hritik Roshan haircut. Young women want to dress as Aishwarya Rai did in a cherished song from *Hum Dil De Chuke Sanam*. Before the current era of designers and beauty pageants, Hindi cinema enjoyed a monopoly in influencing fashion. The clothes worn by early stars were copied by many people, as designer Leena Daru remembers: 'Women would ask their tailors, "Masterji, make a boat-neck sari blouse like the one Nargis wore. Or make me a silk *ghaghara-choli* like Meena Kumari's, or a dress like Madhubala's." People would definitely follow film fashion.'

Akbar Shahpurwallah, who designed Amitabh's look in the 1970s, believes that more than cinema, it is now television that is influencing lifestyle and fashion in cities and small towns:

Akbar Shahpurwallah: Every village has got a television set – that's been the greatest influence. In villages and small towns, boys now want to wear jeans and baggy clothes. Cottons play a very big part, so everybody is changing. In some years, you won't find an Indian traditional look any more for men in this country. For women, it's different. But based on my clientele, nobody wants any Indian styles. Since the explosion of television, everyone is aping the West and dressing like them. Only the foreigners who come here want to wear Nehru jackets, *sherwanis* and have the Indian look.

Audiences may want to change their look, but they expect Hindi cinema to adhere to fixed genres. It is known, for example, that North Indian audiences, especially in small-town Punjab, are keen on the action film. A most popular star in the 1950s and 1960s was actor/wrestler Dara Singh, and following his success, other actors who are regarded as he-men do particularly good business in the small towns of Punjab. In stunt director Mahendra Varma's experience, boxing, fist fights, wrestling and any 'man-to-man fight' has great appeal with audiences. The self-proclaimed 'Bad Man of Hindi Movies', Gulshan Grover, believes the action film's predictability is its main asset:

Gulshan Grover: Action films are considered to be the safest films in the commercial setting. The action scenes in our movies are long because people love action. The audience doesn't believe you can punch someone out in two punches. No, not in our kind of movies. You need to beat the guy again and again and again, he goes down, he comes back again, he fights some more, he falls down. And all this adds to the excitement. If we show a guy being knocked out by one or two punches, as they do in Hollywood movies, the Indian audience will feel cheated. We make films that will be seen in large theatres where the equipment is horrible. In some theatres, you can't even see the film properly and the sound is distorted. That's why our fight scenes have loud sound effects. Every time you punch a guy, you'll hear a huge sound – *pshhh*, *dung*, *daa* and all that. Five hundred prints of a film are distributed in cities and far-off places, in small towns and villages.

One genre that has a steady following in small-town India is the horror movie. This genre favours very similar storylines to Western horror films, although with perhaps less gore and violence. The pioneers of the horror film are the Ramsays – F.U. Ramsay, three of his sons (Tulsi, Shyam and Gangu) and his grandson Deepak – who are considered the kings of the genre. One of their early productions, *Do Gaz Zameen ke Neeche* ('What Lies Beneath') (1975, Tulsi Ramsay), was a major success and established the Ramsays as India's premier horror movie makers. Their films are renowned for their titles, which generally give away half the plot: *Purana Mandir* ('The Old Mansion') (1984, Tulsi Ramsay), *Tower House*, *Guest House* (1980, Tulsi and Shyam Ramsay), and *Hotel* (1981, Tulsi and Shyam Ramsay). At the height of their fame, the Ramsay brothers made films within a budget of 20 to 30 lacs (around £45,000). Their monopoly on the genre was broken, however, when producers who could not afford big stars started to make horror movies with even tinier budgets of 5 to 10 lacs (£15,000) hoping to appeal to C centres (villages or small towns). Small-town distributors soon stopped paying for the Ramsay productions and bought the less classy horror films instead. In order to survive, the Ramsays subsequently began making horror shows for television. Some of these shows, such as Tulsi and Shyam's *Zee Horror* Show, a late-night series on the Zee satellite channel, have proved very popular.

The main appeal of the low-budget horror movie is that it is more overtly sexual and suggestive. Early Indian films contained kissing scenes but these had disappeared by the 1930s. Sex on screen, and kissing for that matter, has become largely a no-go area, something that has been one of the most publicized facts about Indian cinema in the West. Author Kobita Sarkar, a member of the Censor Board for over a decade, writes, 'It is true that there is no legal bar against kissing in Indian cinema, that it did exist once, and its deletion suddenly became a convention that, I feel, has adversely influenced our cinema. Even the female film stars suddenly developed a violent antipathy to the actual kiss in Indian films' (*'You Can't Please Everyone!' Film Censorship: The Inside Story*, IBH Publishing Company, Bombay, 1982). Over the years, some popular films have included a kissing sequence, such as *Satyam Shivam Sundaram* (1978, Raj Kapoor) and *Raja Hindustani* (1996, Dharmesh Darshan), but the idea of no-kissing has become such a tradition in Hindi films (replaced by the 'wet sari dance' and various other forms of physical closeness, particularly those suggested in song), that it now seems an unimaginative form of affection. It is also true that Indian actresses look so uncomfortable kissing their co-stars that the kiss, when it is featured, is bland and self-conscious. Consequently, the male audience looks to horror movies for screen sex. Sexual activity for monsters, ghosts, satanic priests, and demons is simply seen as a natural part of their evil pursuits.

Horror and science-fiction films have not interested many A-list producers, although occasionally a reincarnation or ghost story has achieved great success. Early examples include *Mahal* (1949, Kamaal Amrohi), *Bees Saal Baad* (1962, Biren Naug), *Madhumati* (1958, Bimal Roy) and the ghost story *Jaani Dushman* (1979, Rajkumar Kohli) with top stars Sunil Dutt, Sanjeev Kumar, Shatrughan Sinha, Rekha and Reena Roy. Although these films did well, mostly because of their fabulous music and songs, they did not change the perception that horror movies weren't for big-city audiences. Taran Adarsh, film critic and editor of leading Indian industry magazine *Trade Guide*, looks at why horror movies appeal to rural India:

Taran Adarsh: Horror films don't enjoy a market in the big city because audiences want to see star cast movies and horror films have unknown faces. The business for horror films is limited to small centres. The ghost story has appeal, too. Indians are very superstitious, we believe in a lot of things which Westerners would find outrageous or strange. In India, we talk of reincarnation, we talk of ghosts. Go to any village and people will say, 'Don't go near that tree, there's a ghost there.' It's so common here, that's why audiences in small villages identify with these kind of movies. If you divide the film industry into A, B and C-grade filmmakers, then you'll find it's the C-grade filmmaker who produces films which are a mix of horror and sex – more sex than horror, actually. These films cost nothing and are completed in seven days. The lower classes want to see these films, not for the horror, but for the sleaze and the sex. What attracts the audience in small centres are the 'bits' – those uncensored portions that are added into the print after the censors have cleared the film. I don't think the Censor Board has any control in small centres. They may raid a particular theatre in the city, but what about the 500 or 700 centres all over the country?

The experience of watching the audience react to a Hindi film usually offers more original entertainment than the action on the screen. The greater the popularity of the star, the greater the audience's reaction. In the 1950s, films such as *Albela*, featuring wonderful dances and songs, had people throwing coins at the screen in appreciation of Bhagwan's dance steps. Audiences are also known to recite lines of dialogue along with the actors who voice them. Gabbar Singh's line in *Sholay*, '*Arre O Sambhaa, kitne admi the?*' ('O Sambhaa, how many men were there?') is a case in point. The whole world and his uncle knew that line of dialogue and the moment Gabbar Singh opened his mouth on screen, the audience would prepare themselves to echo his words. Watching a film in India is an interactive experience; front benchers cheer while the villain gets his just desserts and whistle when the heroine performs a sexy dance.

Jaaved Jaaferi: The audience in a cinema hall is divided into different sections: front benches, the stalls and the balcony. The front benchers are people who sit right in the front and go more for the crude stuff, double-meaning dialogues, cat-calling at vulgar movements, thrusting movements of the heroine. They whistle and comment, that's the front bench. The stalls are slightly better and the audience there is the lower-middle class and the middle class. The balcony is usually the upper-middle class. It's amazing, because each section of the audience reacts totally differently to the film.

The front benchers say, 'We have paid and we're going to make it worth our while; if we want to make comments, we will. If we want to scream, we will. If we want to be lewd, we'll do that. It's our birthright to pass comments in this theatre.' Certain movies flop in the A centres and in B centres they do tremendous business. But the mass audience is in the B and C centres. Very few movies run universally. *Mother India*, *Sholay*, and *Hum Apke Hain Koun*, these films appealed to everyone.

Going to the cinema has always been, and continues to be, the cheapest form of entertainment in India. Ticket prices in cinemas that seat 1,500 range from Rs 25 to Rs 100 (£1= Rs 65). For the price of a ticket, the audience gets around three hours of entertainment in a space that's air-conditioned (or at least cooled by many ceiling fans) and buzzing with life and energy. Seats for new and big films are also sold on the 'black' by ticket touts. The way of gauging whether the film or the star is hot with the audience is reflected in how much the tickets sell for on the black market during the first few weeks of the film's release. If a new film has been declared worth seeing, and having repeat value (audiences are known to see a favourite film many times), tickets can sell for five times the usual price to an enthusiastic audience. Actor Manoj Bajpai believes that the reaction of city folk is subdued compared to that of C-centre audiences, who are not afraid to show their emotions:

Manoj Bajpai: I was telling a friend of mine, if you really want to enjoy a Hindi film, you should go to some small town in Bihar. Small-town people tear their shirts when they are feeling very excited. They do that when a hit song is on the screen; when some titillating dance is going on, you see coins been thrown at the screen. It's madness. They don't hold back any emotion, they don't care a damn what people think. If they want to cry, they cry or howl in the theatre.

My sister called me from my home town and said that there was a riot at the box-office for my film *Shool* – the story of the film is based in a small town – and whenever I speak certain dialogues which have to do with the importance of honesty, people relate to it so much – they clap and shout. You can actually experience their emotions, these loud emotions. In cities, audiences go to the theatre with expectations. In small towns, they don't have any expectations, they come to enjoy the film and if you betray them, and you let them down and can't hold them, then you'll see empty theatres the next day. They are extreme in their emotions; the city people aren't – I would say they don't know how to enjoy a Hindi film.

An audience survey outside a busy Bombay cinema reveals a kaleidoscope of perceptions of Bollywood. One young couple comment, 'You leave your mind at home, you come here, get entertained and go home. What Hindi films teach us about life is how to pass time!' A man in his thirties adds, 'It's all the same routine. Two brothers separated, then united, there's romance, the usual. The son always loves his mother, it gets just too emotional. And the son sacrifices his life. That never happens in real life. In real life, girls aren't like the heroines either. Not so forward. Indian audiences are intelligent enough not to believe things that are absolutely unreal.' 'Audiences don't care about how the film is made,' argues a woman in her thirties. 'They don't see the technical and aesthetic things, only the acting and the songs interest them. Girls go to see their favourite heroes, that's it.' A young mother joins in, 'People are very emotional. The family ties you see in Hindi films move us. Hindi films give a lot of importance to relationships. If you see the old Amitabh films, he will do anything for his mother.' 'In the old days, you could buy a ticket for 10 or 12 rupees,' comments a mill worker in his fifties, 'now you have to pay 50 rupees. A man doesn't earn 50 rupees a day, and he saves two days' wages to see a film, so it had better be good.' 'A Hindi movie is a mix of everything,' a young college boy exclaims, adding, 'The only difference between Hollywood and Bollywood is that Hollywood has more reality. Bollywood films have happy endings for happy Indians.'

Director David Dhawan has achieved a lot of success in his career, but knows films have to keep changing with the times:

David Dhawan: That's why people are making modern films; it's a laugh-a-minute riot, you know, and a few tears here and there. And the music is key. Today you need thrills, your songs have to be different, you've got to have lots of dancers, lots of padding and great locations. Today the stories are definitely thinner. And on top of that, if the audience sees a bad song, they get bored, they walk away. In a theatre that seats 1,500, you see 500 people get up at a time and walk out. You've got to be very careful, the pace of the film is very important, scene-to-scene transition is very important.

Just relying on predictability does not work, so you've got to give them something new. Audiences who don't travel outside India see the world on screen. Glamour has become a big thing. And the pace and the tempo of the movies have changed, the action on screen is very fast paced. In the earlier films, you'd see a man come in and sit down, he walks, a car drives in – all those shots have gone. Now you cut to the point, you come to the scene. The audience has changed, their lifestyle, their way of working and living has changed; they can't relate to anything soft and slow any more. Nobody has time today.

One amazing fact about Indian audiences is the speed with which they make up their minds about a film. If a new movie is released on a Friday, by Sunday the audience has decided whether the film is good or bad. The verdict 'This film won't run' spreads within forty-eight hours and the chain reaction of this damning word-of-mouth review is enough to destroy the film. And no matter how much distributors, producers or film critics may then try to promote or recommend the film, it's dead in the water.

There have always been spectacular exceptions to the rule. People still recount the story about how *Sholay* had been written off by the trade press as a non-starter following a lukewarm reaction from the audience. *Sholay* went on to become one of Indian cinema's five top earners of all time. Another example is *Pakeezah,* which only attracted vast crowds after its lead star, Meena Kumari, had died. But *Pakeezah* and *Sholay* are exceptions. In most cases, the lifelong fate of a film is determined by whether the audience on the first day it is released like it or not.

The one actor who has never failed to open successfully is Amitabh Bachchan. He is renowned for his 'initial' draw, and whether audiences like or don't like the film, they will still form long queues for a new Amitabh starrer. The actor himself can no longer enter an Indian cinema (or go anywhere in India for that matter), without being mobbed. But he remembers clearly what seeing a film with an audience was like:

Amitabh Bachchan: I attempted that once. It was when *Zanjeer*, my first successful film, was screened. I'd gone down to the Strand cinema in Colaba. A couple of days before I went to the cinema, some of my friends had taped the audience reactions to the film, and they came and played it back to me. I said, 'No, this is probably just fixed by you guys so maybe I need to go and check it out myself.' Initially, I was quite taken aback. I had to actually sneak in because the theatre managers, who were being very protective, didn't let me walk in like an ordinary man. I found the experience very embarrassing, you know, I didn't think that I was doing something that extraordinary on screen to merit the kind of a reaction

I got. Yes, there was reaction, they were shouting and screaming and stuff like that. It was very encouraging and one felt good about it. Recently, when *Major Saab* was released, and during a song sequence, a friend called me on his mobile from the theatre and said, 'Here, listen! People are dancing in the aisles and throwing money at the screen.' I could hear the cheering on his mobile.

There is a large following for Hindi cinema in the Diaspora and in countries beyond the Indian subcontinent. A new Bollywood film is released simultaneously in all the major cities of the world – this trend started in the 1980s, as distributors were seeking to combat video pirates. The latter were very efficient in making a copy of a new film and selling it on the black market before the film print made its way to London, Dakar or Cairo. Even today, Indian distributors, who control the international circuit, do not see the necessity of subtitling films to attract a wider, or 'whiter', audience. They are confident that they will make their money back thanks to the dedicated following of people of Indian origin who understand Hindi and who have settled throughout the world. Starting in 1998, when Mani Ratnam's *Dil Se* made it to number 6, Bollywood movies regularly make their way into the UK box-office charts. This is solely because of their success in theatres (including a select number of screens in multiplex cinemas) that cater for British Asians. The world of Bollywood seems to fascinate the Western press, but Hindi films are hardly ever released in mainstream cinemas, whether in London, Paris or New York.

Until the early 1990s, Hindi films mainly interested the older generation of Asians settled overseas, but now this love of Bollywood is shared by the second and third generation of Asians. Director/writer Mahesh Bhatt believes that this increased following in the Diaspora is reflective of a psychological change in young Asians:

Mahesh Bhatt: The Asian abroad is getting more assertive. He wants to celebrate his status, he doesn't want to emulate the white man any more, he is not apologetic about his likes and dislikes. He is today unashamedly saying, 'I like *bhangra*, and I like Hindi film music, and I like Shahrukh Khan more than I like Tom Cruise.' He's celebrating his cultural heritage, where his parents came from. A part of him is saying there is no point pretending that he is comfortable with only an alien culture; he can have the best of both worlds. He can have all the comforts and luxuries of the West and yet tune into his *bhajans* or his favourite Hindi film songs. He can maintain a contact with that India which is no longer a geographical territory for him. India is something that exists inside him, in the crevices of his mind and heart. That's why he feels the need to see more and more Hindi films.

It is surprising to discover that despite the vast number of films produced each year, India has the smallest number of cinemas (13,000 including the touring ones) per head of population (currently around 1 billion). In the largest state, Uttar Pradesh, there are still only 500 theatres. Girish Karnad makes the point that 8,000 of the total number of 13,000 cinemas are in fact in South India: '2,700 are in Andhra Pradesh, about 2,400 are in Tamil Nadu, 1,600 in Kerala and 1,400 in Karnataka. So between four southern states, they have a per head distribution of cinemas which is very high compared to North Indian areas.'

> **Shahrukh Khan**: People choose the films they want to see. Out of the 180 Hindi films that are made, only eight do well. So 172 films are rejected straight away. The deciding factor is the audience and they decide to like a film, they decide to like Shahrukh Khan and Kajol or whoever. Indian audiences living in the West seem to like love stories, pretty things, yellow flowers, high-speed action, women in saris, opulence. So producers make films like *Taal*, *Dil to Pagal Hai*, *Kuch Kuch Hota Hai*, *Dilwale Dulhania Lejayenge* and *Hum Apke Hain Koun* in that style. These films did well for Asians abroad. The Indian audience in India is different. I myself am very close-minded about cinema. I think films should not give social messages, or pass value judgments, or tell you what's right and what's wrong. Films should just make you laugh, cry, sing, dance. Have a good time and come back home, that's all.

Audiences basically look to Hindi films for a fun time out, and whether they live in India or in the Diaspora, they expect Bollywood to deliver an inventory of thrills and situations in which family values are affirmed. In the old days, the entire extended family played a part in the narrative. The family and its various members was then replaced by the figure of the mother, who alone became symbolic of the gamut of traditional values. In more recent films, though the mother-figure is still present, she has become more of a friend than an upholder of the old world. So the traditional world and its values are represented through the wedding ceremony, and all the activities that lead up to it and determine it. And so the wedding has been added to the formula, which may include three fights, six songs, two dances or a different mix of the cocktail: two fights, three dances, nine songs and a wedding. Even today, film-goers react to a movie they like with the comment, '*Paisa vasool*' ('Got my money's worth').

Playwright and actor Girish Karnad believes a turning point in India's performing arts came about when the relationship between the spectacle and the spectator changed:

Girish Karnad: The one thing which changed the performing arts forever in India, which very few people pay attention to, is ticketing of shows – the notion that you had to pay for your tickets whereas you never did before. You always had sponsors, the king sponsored, the ministers sponsored, or if you wanted a child, you'd go to the temple and promise God, 'I have four daughters but if I have a son, I'll sponsor a Kathakali performance.' Once the family had their son, they sponsored the performance as promised. Others may have seen that performance and may have donated some money towards it. But no one had to pay to watch as a condition of admission. With the development of the major cities, the real commercial economy of free trade from the British comes into Indian arts. Pay and then you see.

So what happens is your entertainment becomes a commodity that's being sold. As a performer, you were being paid by the Maharajah or the Nawab or the landlord or whoever, so obviously you performed to please him. So it's the buyer who you try to please, even if there are a thousand other people who may have just come along to watch. Then a real shift takes place. If you see a show that you're not paying for, you take aesthetic risks. But when you pay for it, you are involved in a financial risk. So the audience think, 'Well, I have paid 5 rupees, I must get my 5 rupees of entertainment back.' This means I need six songs, two dances, three fights or whatever. That's where the formula starts.

In the 1930s and 1940s, the main audience in India for films was the urban middle class. By the end of the war years, with a sharp fall in agricultural prosperity, hundreds of thousands of people moved from the village to the city. A further population explosion followed Partition in 1947, when millions of families were uprooted and forced to make new homes. In his excellent book *The Idea of India*, Sunil Khilnani describes the effect Partition had on Delhi, Calcutta and Bombay and the severe problems of resettlement it caused: 'Refugees were housed in temporary encampments that became permanent, ramshackle colonies. The poorest haplessly took up whatever empty space they could find: along roads or railway lines, on vacant land and in parks. One definitive trait of the future history of India's cities was established: a steady, irresistible flow of political and economic refugees, settling wherever they could, necessarily oblivious to the niceties of the intentions behind pavements, parks or traffic roundabouts.' (*The Idea of India*, Hamish Hamilton, London, 1997)

In the 1950s, the urban middle-class audiences found themselves in the minority while the new city migrants had a different expectation of cinema. They were not interested in the dilemmas of introverted heroes like Devdas; instead, they wanted entertainment, songs and dances – and if their difficult lives were reworked in the movies, these reflections had to be romanticized. Audiences preferred Raj Kapoor's vision of the innocent villager (dressed like Chaplin's tramp) in *Shree 420*, who comes to Bombay to make his fortune, rather than Bimal Roy's more realistic *Do Bigha Zameen*, the hero of which arrives in Calcutta and ends up losing everything he has. In *Shree 420*, the hero is seen to turn his back on the corrupting influences of the big city and revert back to values learned in the village.

Rural audiences have fantasies about what life is like in cities and many of these are based on Hindi cinema's representations of the metropolis, and in most cases that means Bombay. However, a rural audience is quick to spot any idealization of village life. Anthropologists Beatrix Pfleiderer and Lothar Lutze have written a fascinating study of how movies are perceived in rural India, in which they note, '...the medium of film, of course, as a cultural product is not rooted in the villages; it is clearly an urban phenomenon. In the popular Hindi film, village life is depicted as the world "outside" or the world where "our roots lie". But this is an urban reflection. It does not reproduce the villagers' needs, neither emotional nor aesthetic. For them, the medium of film represents the "outside world" which has no relationship to their own social and psychic world.' (*The Hindi Film*, Manohar, Delhi, 1985)

India has been going through huge economic and cultural change since the early 1990s. The economy has opened up to the West, and television, cable and satellite channels have mushroomed. Rupert Murdoch's Star channels, beamed from Hong Kong, started this ever-growing trend that also included BBC World, CNN, Zee, Sony, Discovery Channel, MTV and Channel V (a music channel modelled on MTV that has provided a platform for Indian bands). Film distributors who were, in the 1980s, fearful of losing out to the video boom, now experience a real threat from television. In the early 1990s, Indian viewers suddenly had a wide choice of home entertainment. American and British imports such as *The Bold and the Beautiful* (which had all the ingredients of a Hindi film in which long-lost family members are united once again), and *Yes, Minister* became remarkably popular. But in the early years, the highest ratings were reserved for programmes that showed film song clips – what were known as 'film-based programmes', like *Chitrahaar* and *Superhit Muqabala*. Rather than diminishing the impact of Hindi films, television has managed to increase its reach to villages and remote areas that previously depended on the whims of touring cinema operators – so the audience for the movies has never been as widespread, despite the increased competition.

By the 1980s, television producers began to extend choice further by making a greater variety of shows looking beyond the film-based format, and these included soaps such as *Khandaan*, *Hum Log* and *Buniyaad*, and religious dramas including the *Ramayan* and the *Mahabharat*. In the 1990s, sing-along shows, music contests, talent contests, music and award shows have also secured massive audiences. Television has played a great part in changing the social fabric of India, as many popular soaps like *Tara* and *Saans* boldly deal with subjects such as divorce, infidelity, and other subjects that were considered taboo or too risky for cinema. There are many Oprah Winfrey-type shows in which live audiences debate all kinds of domestic and social problems that would never have been discussed previously in such an open and public way. There is also the current craze for the quiz show, such as *Kaun Banega Crorepati*. All these programmes have come to change people's views of what they expect of entertainment.

Rohan Sippy is the son of the director Ramesh Sippy, who made the famous *Sholay*. Twenty-five years after the release of this unforgettable film, Rohan Sippy is about to make his first film, titled *Kuch na Kaho*, to be released in 2002 and starring Abhishek Bachchan. The young director remembers going to the set of *Sholay* as a child and being thrilled to see Amitabh Bachchan 'in the flesh'. Rohan Sippy realizes all too well how many new challenges a young filmmaker in India faces today as the lifestyles and aspirations of the audience change. He is also aware that many among the growing middle classes would be just as happy not to go to the cinema, but to stay home and browse on the internet.

Rohan Sippy: One of the main challenges that we face, like many producers of goods and services in various Indian industries, is that the market is opening up. We are facing more and more competition through new media, satellite television and on top of that, international films are seen here more than before. We have to retain our link with our audience, but at the same time this makes it more difficult to break out and do

something new. But we must remember that audiences are less likely to see a 'relatively' shoddy Hindi action film if *Matrix II* is running in the same multiplex. Obviously, on a technical level, things are improving all the time in India, but all these advancements in technical processes come with their baggage. Getting command over them means you spend more and more time on technique, and less on concentrating on the soul of filmmaking – performance. And unless you have a wizard like music director Rahman at the wheel, increase in technical choice is a double-edged sword.

In recent years, government restrictions on the number of foreign films entering India have been lifted, but foreign films still have a limited appeal, catering mainly to an English-speaking city audience. Bollywood wins comfortably over Hollywood in terms of Indian audiences, although Hollywood has tried to break into this lucrative market by dubbing films into Hindi. So far only the Hindi version of *Jurassic Park* has had the kind of returns at the box-office that an Indian film such as Karan Johar's *Kuch Kuch Hota Hai* has achieved. This successful young director is currently busy filming his second film, *Kabhi Khushi Kabhi Gham* ('Sometimes There's Happiness, Sometimes Sorrow') in India and in Britain. It is rumoured to be the most expensive Hindi film ever made, and is scheduled for release at Diwali, 2001. The film has a most impressive line-up of top stars, including Amitabh Bachchan, Shahrukh Khan, Hritik Roshan, Jaya Bachchan, Kajol, and Kareena Kapoor; the music is said to be wonderful and the story full of emotion. Karan Johar is completely positive about the future of Hindi cinema:

> **Karan Johar:** You may have fifty TV channels but the magic of cinema in our country or anywhere else in the world will never disappear. Going to the cinema to see a film is the main form of entertainment in India. How long will you sit at home and watch TV? People love watching films in the cinema-hall – buying their popcorn, missing the beginning, rushing in, then going out at the interval for *chai* and coffee, and then coming back home and discussing the film and the stars and how they performed. The lively discussions that follow the movie are even more entertaining to the audience than the film itself. Which star was good, who wasn't; the songs were shot well or they weren't shot well. That kind of discussion is what every Indian lives for. The magic of the entire experience of cinema will always remain.

Indian cinema, which started its story in the mythological and the Urdu Parsee Theatre nearly one hundred years ago, is still bold and buoyant. Its loyal audience will never tire of its mix of song, action, love, glamour, family values, lovely clothes and beautiful people. It represents an ideal world which is, in part, what the movies are all about. A young Asian girl at a cinema in the Midlands specializing in showing Indian movies, turns to her friend and says in a strong Birmingham accent, 'Life seems so easy in Hindi films, doesn't it?' Her friend, looking into the distance, answers wistfully, 'Yeah, it does.'

INDEX